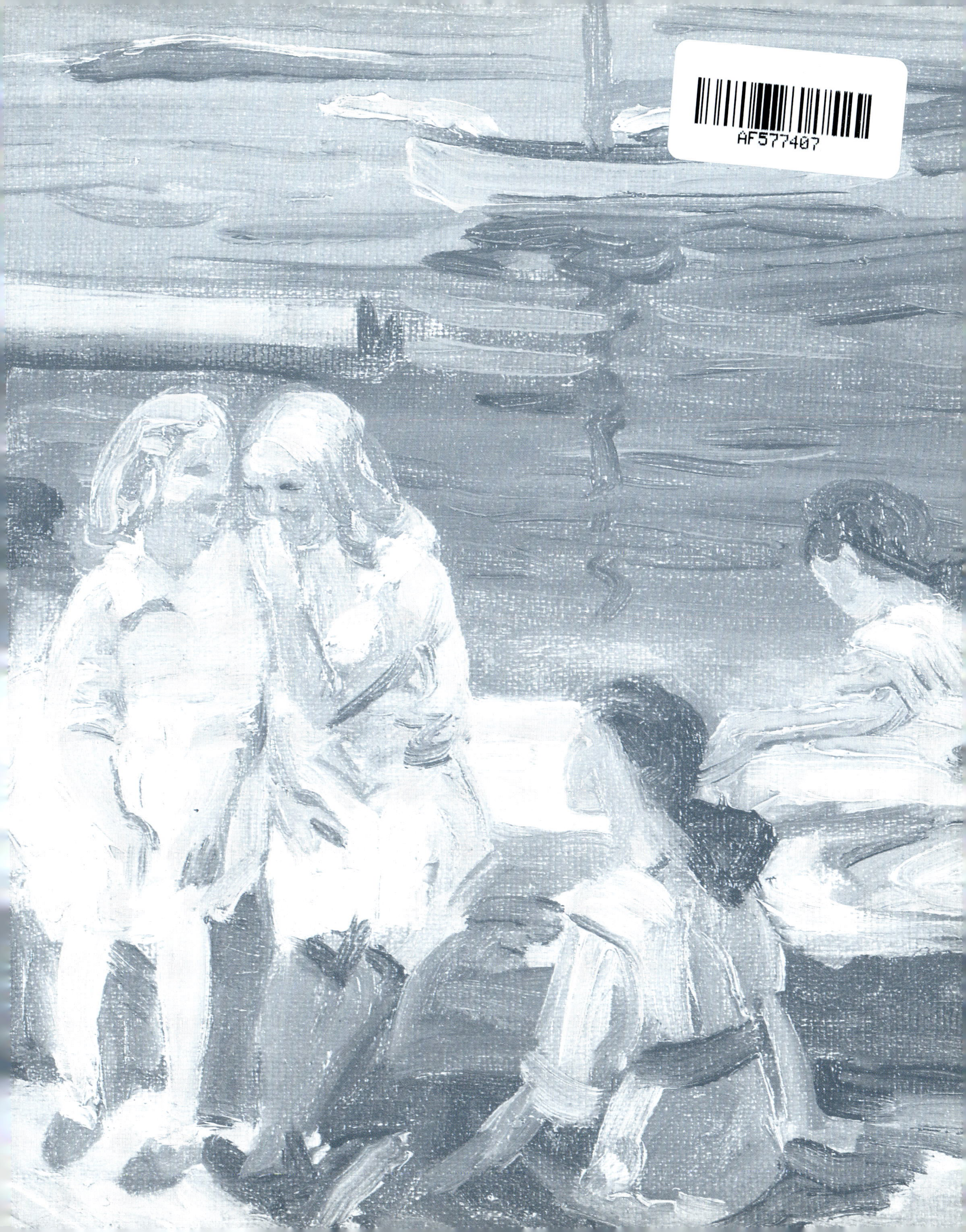

# Before 1948

*American Paintings in Georgia Collections*

# BEFORE 1948

## *American Paintings in Georgia Collections*

CURATORS
*Donald D. Keyes and Heidi Domescik*

WITH AN INTRODUCTION BY
*Terry Kay*

CATALOGUE ENTRIES BY
*Heidi Domescik and Donald D. Keyes*

PROJECT EDITOR
*Jennifer DePrima*

GEORGIA MUSEUM OF ART • UNIVERSITY OF GEORGIA

Cover: Catalogue number 40
Frontispiece: Catalogue number 31

Inside details: page 2-3, catalogue number 31; page 6, catalogue number 50; page 8, catalogue number 27; page 12, catalogue number 25; page 66-67, catalogue number 39


*Before 1948: American Paintings in Georgia Collections*
January 15-March 14, 1999



Design: Kimberly Adis
Department of Publications: Bonnie Ramsey and Jennifer DePrima
Editorial Intern: Hillary Brown

Printed in an edition of 2000 by Friesens
Printed in Canada

Generous support for this catalogue was provided by the Forward Arts Foundation, Atlanta. Additional support for this exhibition and catalogue has been provided by Belk and Southland Auctions Inc., Atlanta and by Director's Circle members Mrs. Edith V. Jordan and Mr. and Mrs. Chester A. Roush, Jr. Partial support for the exhibitions and programs for the Georgia Museum of Art is provided by the Georgia Council for the Arts through appropriations of the Georgia General Assembly. Individuals, foundations, and corporations provide additional support through their gifts to the University of Georgia Foundation.

Library of Congress Cataloging-in-Publication Data
Before 1948: American Paintings in Georgia Collections/general editor, Donald D. Keyes ;
with an introduction by Terry Kay; catalogue entries by Heidi Domescik and Donald D. Keyes.
p. cm.
Catalogue of an exhibition held at the Georgia Museum of Art, University of Georgia,
Jan. 15-Mar. 14, 1999
Includes bibliographical references.
ISBN 0-915977-36-2
1. Painting, American — Exhibitions. 2. Painting — Collectors and collecting —
Georgia — Exhibitions. I. Keyes, Donald D. II. Domescik, Heidi. III. Georgia Museum of Art.
ND205.B43 1999
759.13'074'75818—dc2198-30571 CIP

# Table of Contents

ACKNOWLEDGMENTS *9*
*William U. Eiland*

BEFORE 1948 *9*
*Donald D. Keyes*

GIVING WAY *13*
*Terry Kay*

CATALOGUE OF THE EXHIBITION *23*
*Heidi Domescik and Donald D. Keyes*

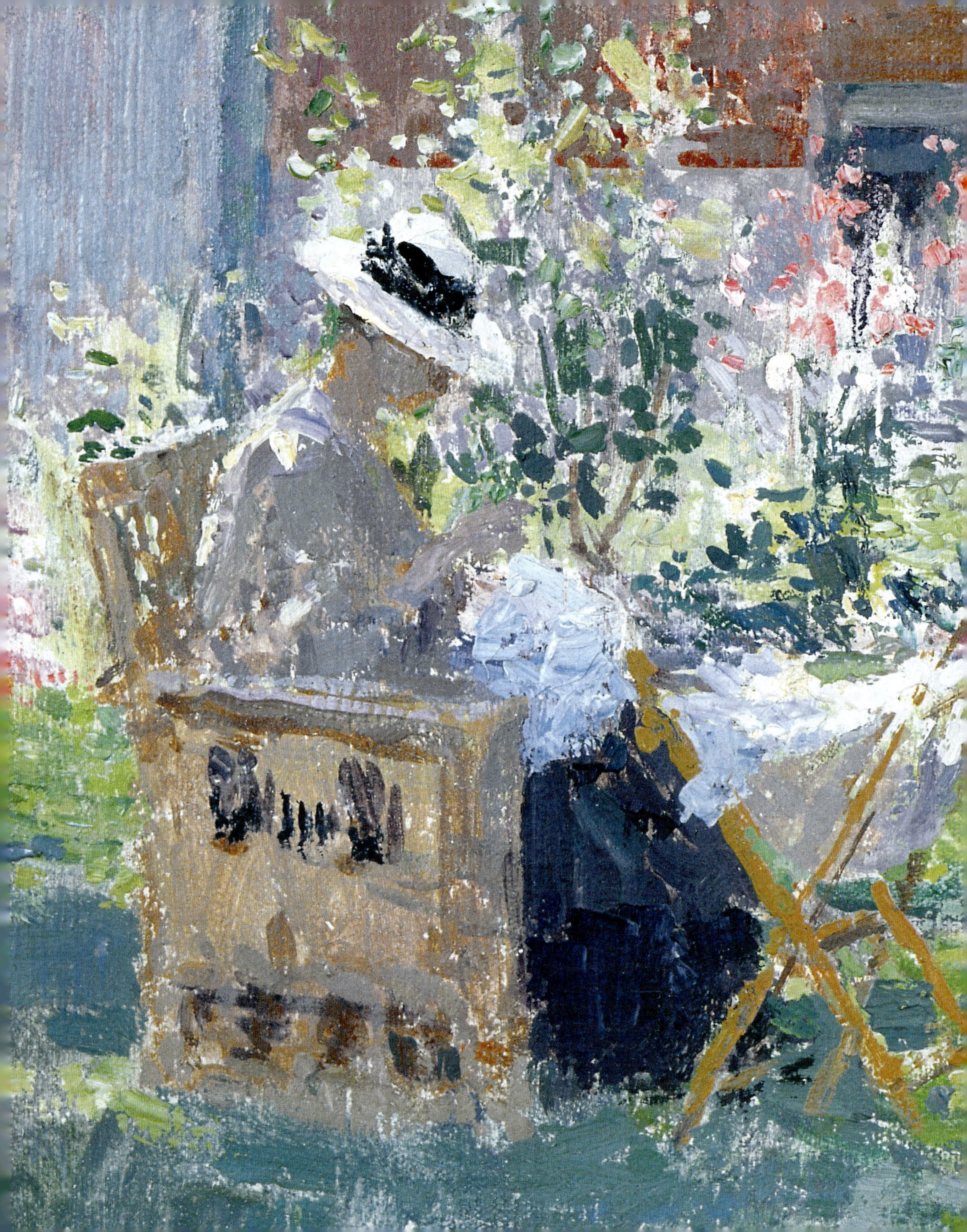

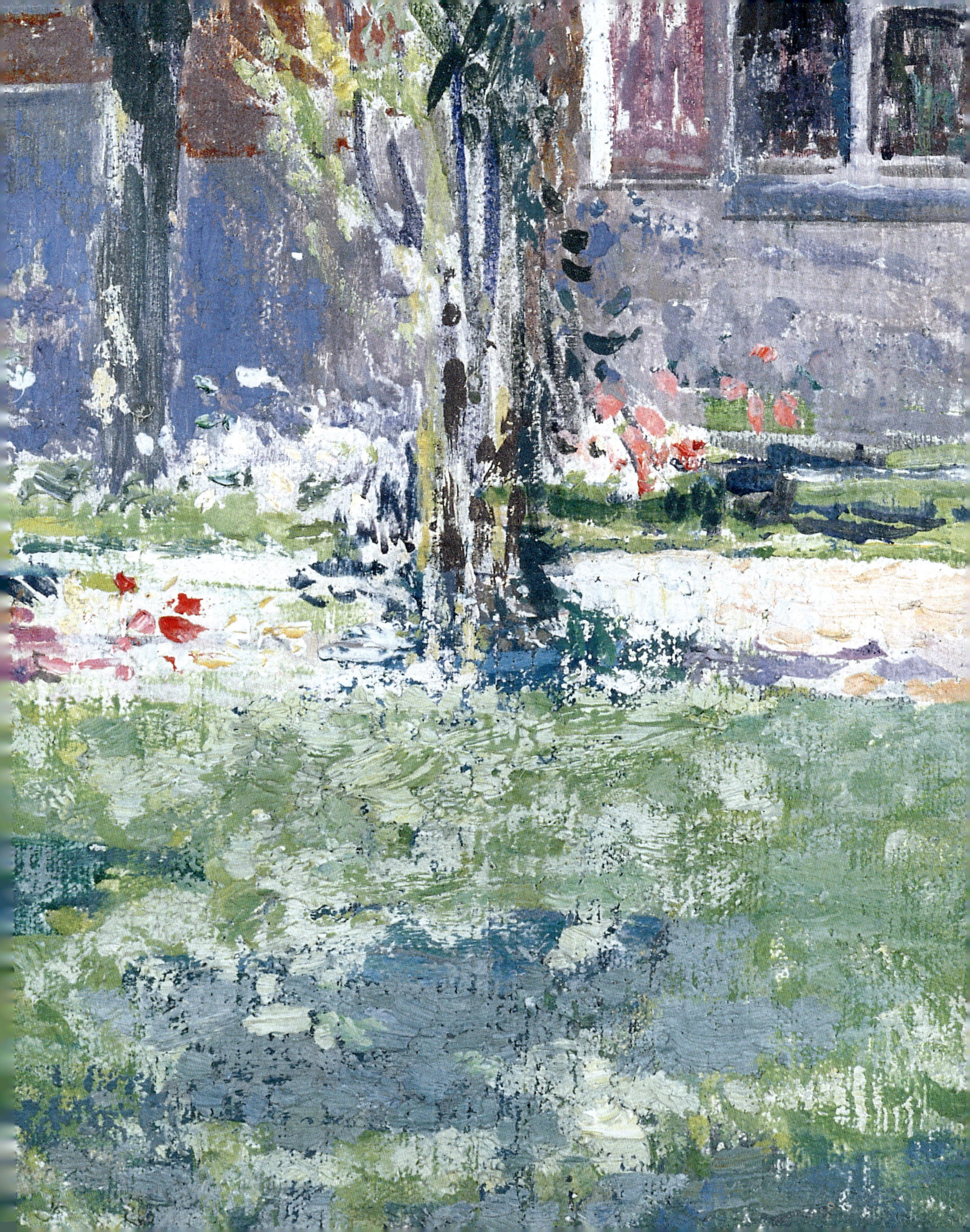

# Lenders to the Exhibition

*Albany Museum of Art*

*Mr. and Mrs. Fred D. Bentley, Sr.*

*Mr. and Mrs. R. Randall Bentley, Sr.*

*Beverly Hart Bremer*

*Mr. and Mrs. Otis T. Brumby*

*The Columbus Museum*

*Dr. and Mrs. Tom Cooper*

*Mr. and Mrs. Henry D. Green*

*Mr. and Mrs. Holcombe Green*

*Barbara Guillaume Griffin*

*Mary Ann Rogers Hammaker*

*Kathryn W. Hartzog*

*High Museum of Art*

*Heather C. Huber*

*Mr. and Mrs. Jack Huber*

*Mr. and Mrs. Dave Knoke*

*Mrs. Edward L. McConnell*

*Mark and Lynn McConnell*

*Mr. and Mrs. David E. Miller, Jr.*

*C.L. Morehead, Jr.*

*Morris Museum of Art*

*Private Collection*

*The Sellars Collection*

*Stephen and Linda Sessler*

*Mrs. Deen Day Smith*

*Terry and Margaret Stent*

*Dr. and Mrs. Jeb Stewart*

*Telfair Museum of Art*

*Mr. and Mrs. Noel Wadsworth*

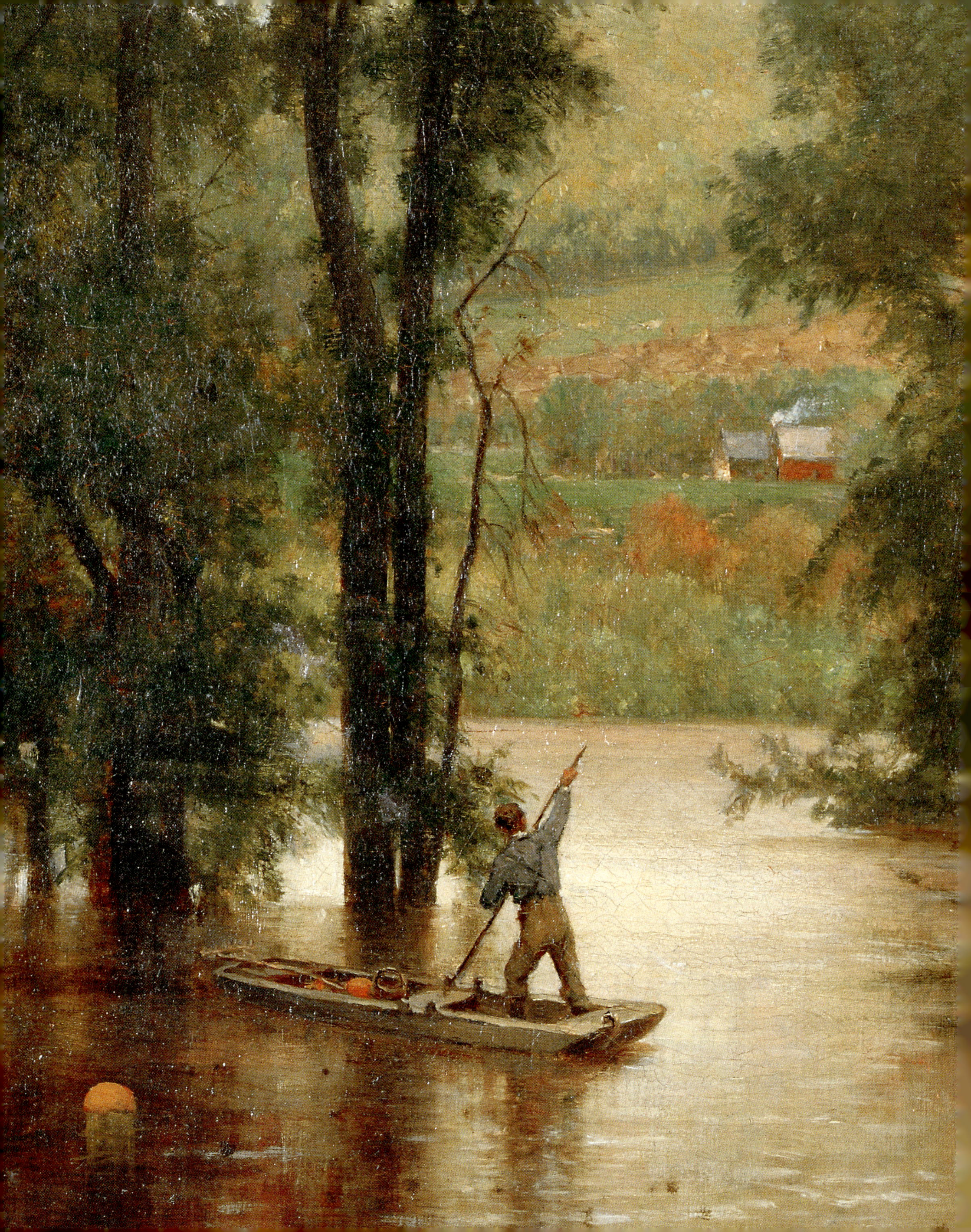

# Sponsor

The Forward Arts Foundation is privileged to participate in the celebration of the Georgia Museum of Art's fiftieth anniversary through our sponsorship of this magnificent catalogue.

Since its founding in 1967 by twelve distinguished Atlanta arts patrons, the Forward Arts Foundation has provided serious volunteer efforts to help create and inspire the modern cultural climate of Atlanta. In commemoration of this half-century anniversary, the Foundation broadens, for the first time in our history, our support of the visual arts in Atlanta to salute a statewide organization that shares our vision of the crucial role of the arts in the lives of Georgians.

Our sponsorship is the emphatic endorsement of the Museum's accomplishments in the education and elevation of the consciousness of the many facets of art. We dedicate this catalogue to the Georgia Museum of Art for its successful influence in the preservation and presentation of the visual arts and generating excitement and enthusiasm for Georgia's arts environment.

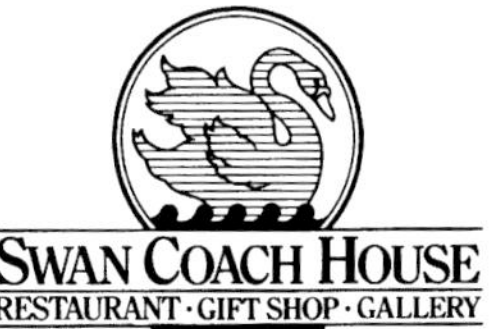

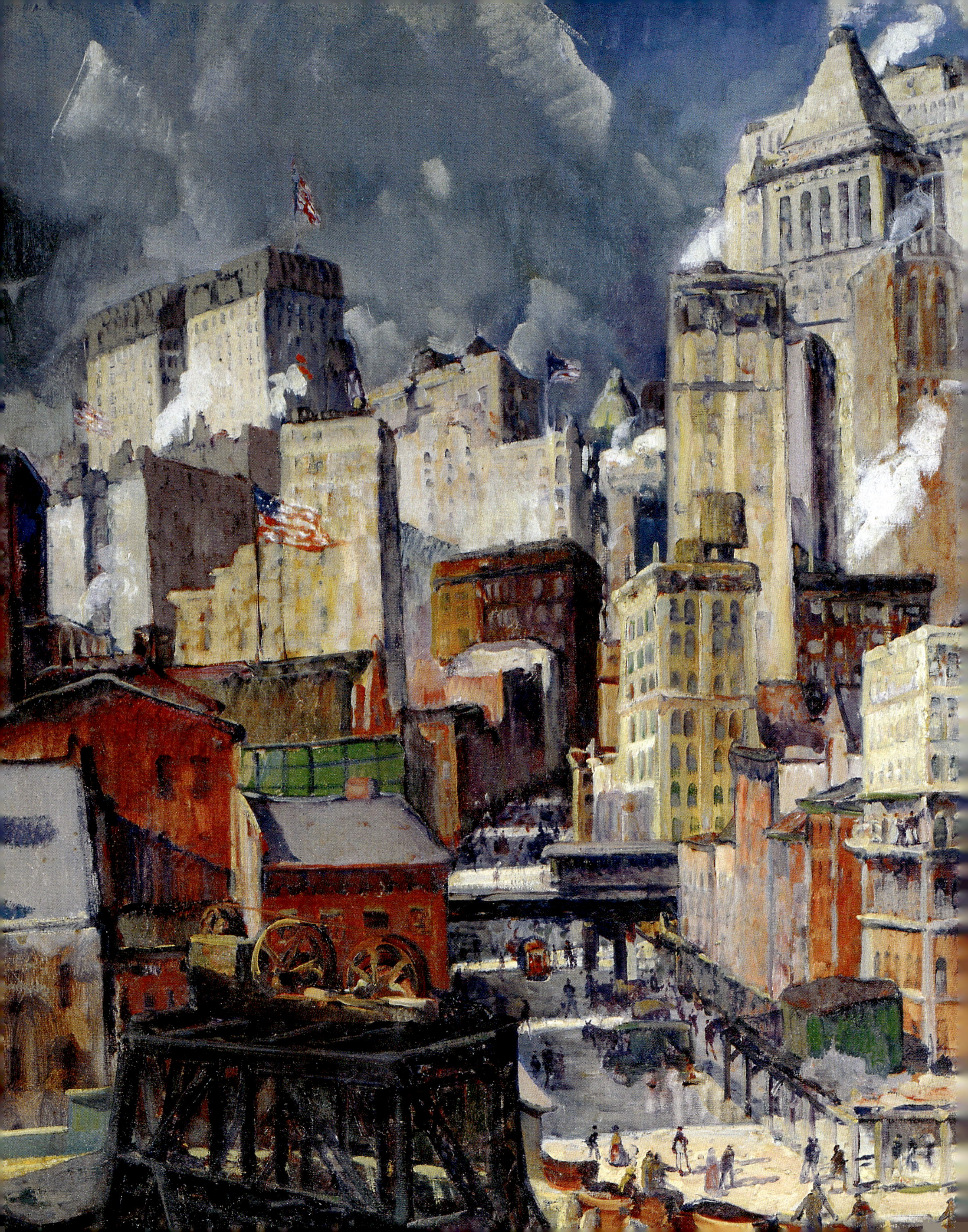

# Acknowledgments

In his essay for this catalogue, Terry Kay recalls the years in rural Georgia before 1948: "I think of those years fondly, as the best years, years of my Age of Innocence, before innocence gave way to experience, before I began my own exodus." In some ways, that same year was the age of innocence for the Georgia Museum of Art as it opened its doors for the first time to the public and to the university community it was destined to serve. In the fifty years since, its innocence has also given way to experience as it, too, began its exodus from a small, provincial museum to an academic museum of national and international repute.

This exhibition and catalogue commemorate those first fifty years of experience by honoring the collectors of Georgia, who have grown in sophistication along with the museum. Alfred Heber Holbrook, the founder and first director of the Georgia Museum of Art, stressed direct education; he believed that the object mattered, that the contemplation of a work of art and the viewer's enjoyment of that work led to a personal aesthetic not restricted to a scholarly or urban audience. Everyone, according to Holbrook, could develop not only an appreciation of the visual arts but also a deeper understanding of his own humanity through the nearness of beauty.

Mr. Holbrook would join the current staff of the museum in applauding the generosity of the lenders to this exhibition; he would be equally appreciative of the students and staff who participated directly in its preparation. Certainly he would be as thankful as we are to the patrons, Belk, Temme Barkin-Leeds and Sally Faulkner, directors of Southland Auctions Inc., Atlanta, Edith V. Jordan, and Mr. and Mrs. Chester A. Roush, Jr., who were generous in their support of this project. We are honored to dedicate this catalogue to the Forward Arts Foundation of Atlanta for their generous sponsorship. We acknowledge them with gratitude.

This anniversary is but one milepost on that exodus which Terry Kay describes so well, a journey of both adventure and promise, and, most important, one of service. For this reason, we celebrate our audiences, past, present, and future, as they travel along with us.

William U. Eiland

*Director, Georgia Museum of Art*

# Introduction

This exhibition and catalogue celebrate the fifty years that the Georgia Museum of Art has been open to the public. Inspired by Alfred Heber Holbrook's generosity and affection for American art, the museum has grown from his collection of one hundred American paintings displayed in the basement of the former university library to one of the premier arts institutions in Georgia.

During World War II, Holbrook retired to Athens, drawn mainly by its quiet charm and the opportunity to study in the growing department of art. As demonstrated in Terry Kay's essay, the region may have seemed ripe for Holbrook to make a significant contribution with his collection and to provide a new life for him following a distinguished legal career and the death of his wife. Holbrook's small collection of paintings steadily grew during the last twenty-five years of his life in Athens.

As Terry Kay also discusses, what may seem like an era of celebration and triumph of American ideals was actually a period of complex changes. During the museum's first years the Berlin Blockade took place while the Iron Curtain was descending across Central Europe, Senator Joseph McCarthy and the House Un-American Activities Committee were zealously pursuing Communists and their purported sympathizers, Jackson Pollock was being touted as a purveyor of the new American freedom in art, African Americans were demanding equality and, in 1961,

*"What was truly innovative about Holbrook was his attraction to the art of his lifetime, American realism and modernism of the first half of the twentieth century."*

entrance to the University of Georgia, and television was coming of age.

At the time Holbrook was collecting, European art dominated the Western art world, and only works by Colonial artists, Thomas Eakins, Winslow Homer, Albert Pinkham Ryder, and John Singer Sargent were deemed worthy of the serious collector. The earliest paintings in Holbrook's collection were drawn from the country's first indigenous artistic movement, the Hudson River school, which was not limited to the Hudson River region of New York nor to a proper or formal school. This movement, beginning in the 1830s and continuing until after the Civil War, featured landscape painting as both recorded fact and as patriotic and religious ideal. Holbrook's collecting acumen really stands out in the acquisition of works by artists who were at the time less appreciated (and accordingly priced), beginning with American Impressionism. What was truly innovative about Holbrook was his attraction to the art of his lifetime, American realism and modernism of the first half of the twentieth century. Occasionally, he knew the artists themselves and often purchased works directly from their galleries.

The selection for this exhibition stops in 1948, when the museum opened to the public; hence, it does not include the work of what would have been the avant garde for Holbrook, Abstract Expressionism, nor any Post-modern work. A knowledgeable amateur, Holbrook acquired art because he loved it and its creators. Holbrook's attraction to American artists reflects the general population's strong support for nativism and the general distrust of things foreign and alien.

The exhibition loosely follows Holbrook's collecting philosophy, with the museum's opening date serving as the end-date for the featured works. Adhering to Holbrook's early inclination as a collector, folk art, decorative and minor arts, works on paper, and photography are excluded. Several characteristics stand out about the selection of works for this exhibition, aside from the paintings that could not be borrowed. The first is the comparative strength of Holbrook's collection of early modernist works, i.e., paintings from the first half of the century. This exhibition is a tribute to Holbrook's courageous collecting in the 1940s and reflects the predilection of present-day collectors in Georgia for more naturalistic and less abstract art. Holbrook's purchases of American modern art in the early 1940s is all the more remarkable since nearly no one else in the South at the time was doing it. Only with Atlanta's economic boom in the 1960s did the collecting of modern art begin in earnest, but by then contemporary art was far removed from Holbrook's interests. The second characteristic of the exhibition's selection is the general absence of Colonial and Federal paintings in Georgia collections. This lacuna may be partially explained by the widespread destruction of property during the Civil War and the inclination of the region's predominately agrarian population for decorative art: that is, not paintings.

For the catalogue, Terry Kay has written an essay describing his youth near Vanna, Georgia, in what I, an urban Yankee, might term "the middle of nowhere." My family had television in our den about the time Kay's family got electricity. For him, 1948 is alive with wonders; for me it is an historic marker. He communicates with rich clarity what it was like in rural northeast Georgia when the museum was founded, and Athens represented the city and Atlanta a quasi-alien culture. He also brings to a museum catalogue what is so often lacking: writing as a spirited art form.

With this exhibition and catalogue the museum also celebrates a half-century of service to the people of Georgia. The exhibition and catalogue join the museum's continuing recognition of the state's collectors. *Georgia's Legacy*, produced in celebration of the university's bicentennial, was followed by exhibitions of the collection of Dr. Robert P. Coggins and, two years later, Mr. and Mrs. Fred D. Bentley, Sr. During this time, the museum displayed its collection of American art in Washington, D.C., and then in Athens with the exhibition *Forty Years of Collecting: American Paintings, Drawings, and Watercolors from the Georgia Museum of Art.* Not long after came *American Impressionism in Georgia Collections* and the following year *The Hudson River School in Georgia Private Collections.* The museum's recognition of the collector's instinct never stops, as Holbrook would have wished it.

This exhibition would not have taken place without the superlative dedication and perspicacity of Heidi Domescik, a graduate student in art history at the Lamar Dodd School of Art. She worked with the lenders, conducted research, and wrote about the paintings in the exhibition. Margaret Casey and Kristine Potter, interns in the department of paintings, assisted her in the research for the catalogue.

As is so often the case, the lenders, private and public, are the linchpin for the success of an exhibition. All have gone out of their way to make possible our enjoyment of the bounty of their efforts. To the private lenders especially, the museum and staff are grateful because they part, briefly, with irreplaceable treasures.

The staff of the Georgia Museum of Art, as always, has attended to the innumerable details of the exhibition with patience and dedication.

DONALD D. KEYES
*Curator, Department of Paintings*

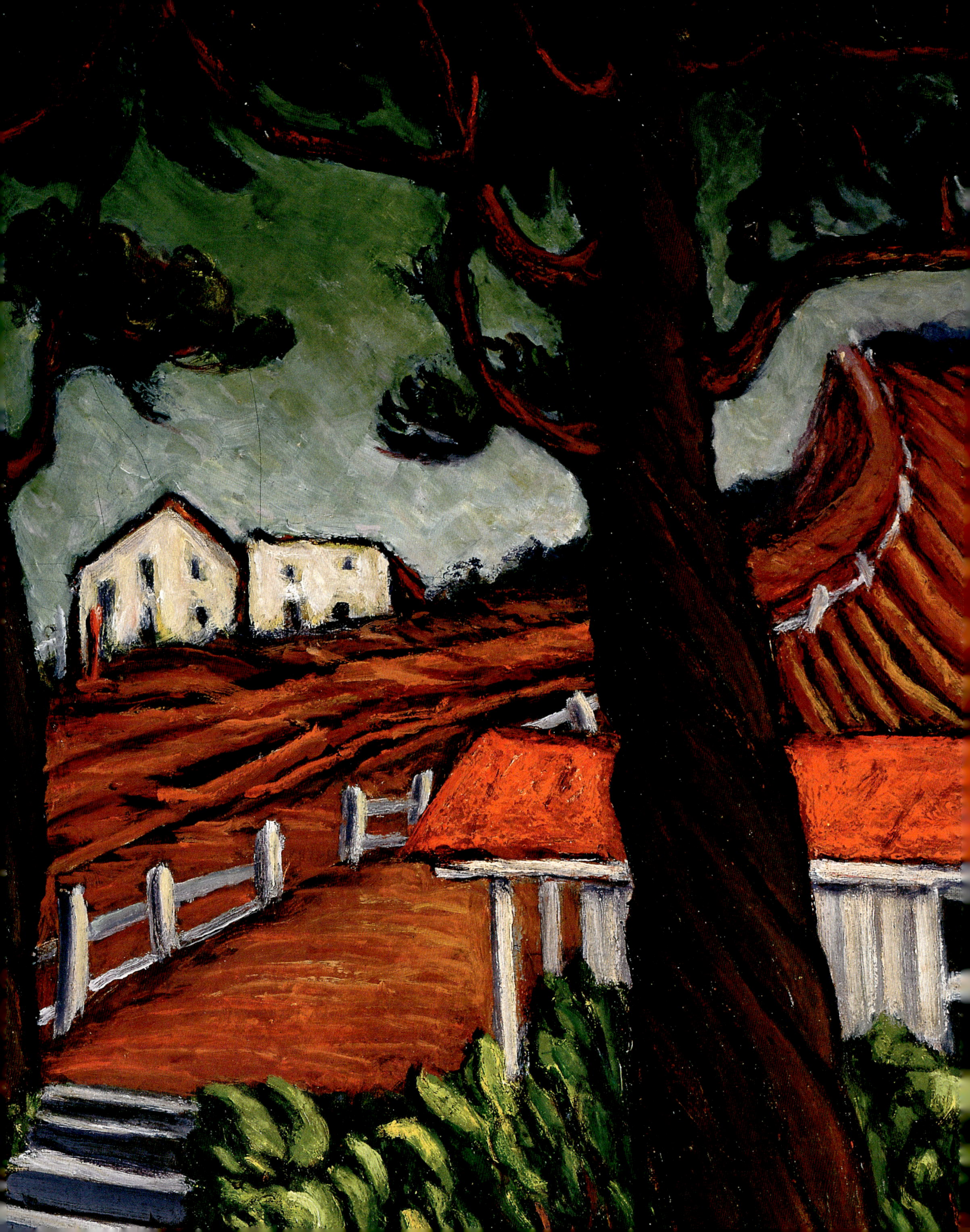

# Giving Way

THE HOUSE SITS ON A KNOLL OFF Viola Winn Road leading to Beaverdam Creek, a half-mile or so from the home of my childhood. Viola Winn Road is named for my mother. Winn was her maiden name.

Once, drooping boughs of large oaks shaded the house. A few shrubs were tucked neatly against it. The dirt yard was always swept clean by hand-made twig brooms. Chinaberry trees grew in the side yard. Peach trees, too, I think. Peach trees that bore nubby peaches. A well for drawing water was between the house and the barn. Chickens promenaded over the grounds, clucking, claw-scratching for bugs, pecking aimlessly. Dogs slumbered in the shade, blowing dust with their breathing. In spring, the air was scented with sassafras and pine and fruit blossoms. In summer, perfume from honeysuckle seeped up from the pasture. In winter, a cold wood musk–a water musk–floated in from the creek and the swamp.

The house is important to me, personally and professionally.

It is the model for every tenant-sharecropper house, every rural setting, I have ever written about.

It is deserted now. Has been for many years. The front porch has fallen away and it has a cracked backbone on the roof line and it is waiting for the vines of poison ivy and fox grape to put it down. Can't see it from the roadbed for so many vines and the trash trees and saw briars and privet bushes growing wild and lush.

Snakes live there. You know it without seeing or hearing them. Snakes hiding in dust and grass in perfect-O curls of cold-blooded muscle. Rats, too. Or maybe not. Maybe the snakes have feasted on the rats.

I wish the house could talk, but it cannot. Time has taken the talk out of it, all the words spilled from broken-out windows and doors. Some floated up the rock chimney, I would guess. Some seeped through floor cracks. Some wiggled out where tongue-and-groove walls used to be, wiggled around heart-pine studs, through rough-planed clapboards.

If the house could talk, I would make a sitting-down place near it–away from the snakes–and ask questions I've always wanted to ask.

The Careys lived there. And before them, the Cromers. Before them, the Harts. Before them, the Carters. Before them, the Humans. Before them, the Crafts.

It was one of the Carter boys who used to sing about finding his thrill on Blueberry Hill to my sister, Nell.

Or so goes the story.

Spied on her from the house, the gossip has it, and when she would go from our home to check the mailbox at the cemetery turnaround–expecting letters from her gone-away boyfriend–he would amble out across the field, crooning his Blueberry Hill love song.

Or so goes the story.

I do not remember the Harts or the Carters

or the Humans or the Crafts. Barely remember the Cromers.

The Careys I remember.

Most of them, at least.

Wallace, Martin, Marie. And there were others. Twins, I think. A boy named Laron. An older daughter, who, like Marie, was remarkably beautiful. Gladys. I believe her name was Gladys. She lived away somewhere, and would come for visits that made for gladness among the Careys. Maybe that was her name: Gladness.

Wallace was older than I. Four years older. The first person I ever idolized. More man than boy, he seemed. Fiercely proud. So much pride it radiated from him in a bright aura that could have been the polished armor of a knight. When we had chinaberry war-games, I would put myself near him, behind his back, and watch in awe. Green-berry bullets, hard as creek pebbles, zipped away with the rubber-snap of his flip. Yelp of someone across the yard, taking the berry in the chest–or back. Wallace would have driven off the Huns with his flip and a fistful of chinaberries. I have written of him in bits and pieces. The bits and pieces are all heroic.

I knocked Martin's tooth out one afternoon in an anger-fit. He had called my dog, Red, a son of a bitch, which was right, technically speaking, but sounded bad enough for a fight.

Someone told me years ago that Marie and her husband had gone to Alaska in search of gold. I hope so. I hope they found a wheelbarrow load of nuggets the size of bricks. It would have been a great adventure for a pretty girl who was reared in a sharecropper's house on a sharecropper's farm.

If the house could talk, I would ask it to tell me if Marie, as a child, had dreamed of finding gold buried under the red clay of cotton fields.

I do not know when the Careys moved from the house, or if they were the last to occupy it. I am certain the family still lived there when I went away to college in the mid-'50s. I know only that on some visit home, I realized the house was empty.

*"Change was everywhere, merrily evolving. It was like being in the middle of a county fair with the snappy blaring of calliope music beating against you."*

In college, professors of sociology were telling us that things were popping. Change was everywhere, merrily evolving. It was like being in the middle of a county fair with the snappy blaring of calliope music beating against you. So much going on, it was impossible to see everything, and everything was tempting.

You had to look carefully to see change, the professors said. Best to pick one thing and watch it. Then you'd see.

I began to look carefully at deserted sharecropper houses on drives over country roads, houses like the one where the Careys once lived.

There was a sameness about them. Unpainted clapboard, bleached gray by rain and sun. Some wrapped in tarpaper. All with a tin roof water-stained the color of tobacco juice.

Yard clutter. Leaf drifts against porch steps. Hand-dug wells covered with cement slabs. Kudzu gone mad.

One of my professors had called change a giving-way thing, and that is what I saw while looking carefully at deserted sharecropper houses:

The mule giving way to the tractor.

The grain thrasher giving way to the combine.

The cotton-mop giving way to the airplane duster.

The field hand giving way to the cotton picker.

The kerosene lamp giving way to the electric light.

The radio giving way to the television.

The row crop giving way to chicken houses.

And the sharecroppers giving way to town houses, giving way to age, giving way to jobs in textile mills, or on the pipe line, or in repair shops, giving way to migrations that would carry them away from memories of long, sun-sapping days in worked-out fields. Sharecroppers giving way to the paycheck, knowing the paycheck–no matter how small–was not as risky as the summing-up of shares.

In college, the professors gave it a word: *Decentralization.* It was one of the things of change, and it meant the breakdown of the unit system–family, community, region, state. (I always thought of it as being *deboned*, taking out the skeleton that held everything together.)

Because of this decentralization, there were remarkable and possibly grave things ahead, the professors predicted. All you had to do was take a look at what had happened since the start of World War II.

The war, the professors declared, had given change a boot in the pants. All that new technology. The atomic bomb. People playing with rockets with thoughts of the moon in their mind. Everything. If the Great Depression had numbed people, the war had put a jolt into them.

And I think they were right. Giving it a backward look, at an age when backward looks have perfect vision or perfect illusion, I think they knew what they were talking about.

During the war, we watched gliders being pulled across American skies by four-motored airplanes, and we wondered what would happen if one of the gliders snapped free of its tether and began to ride the wind above us. Would it circle peacefully like a buzzard and skim to a landing on the white runway of cotton rows? Or would it drop like a rock and splinter into a million pieces of balsa wood?

At play, we fought the Japs and Germans with tree-limb guns and dirt-clod hand grenades, made rifle-firing, pinging-off-rock ricochet sounds in our mouth, held the enemy at bay from foxholes of gullies, and rushed machine gun nests through scrub pine and mountain laurel. Took hits ourselves, of course. Never fatal, of course. Just hits. Nicks. Barely enough to draw blood. Something a saw briar would make.

We collected scrap iron–plow points, railroad spikes, tin cans–to be made into tanks and submarines and anti-aircraft shells the size of our legs. It was kill or be killed, and everyone knew it. The steel plow beam of a middle-buster from a Georgia field might be the very thing that turned the tide in a close fight with the Nazis somewhere in France, or with the Nips on a tiny Pacific island.

The day that Franklin Delano Roosevelt died, I heard it from Cousin Allie Skelton, who came rushing from her home, wailing, "The President's dead, the President's dead!" We were playing in the yard, joyfully whirling in circles on a spinning jenny, and the shriek of that surprising news terrified us. The only picture more prominent than Franklin Delano Roosevelt in rural homes

*"Poetically, I think of it as an exodus of slow-moving people – farm to town, town to city, one state to another, generation following generation, leaving behind gravestones that carry the codes of a personal, yet dim, history."*

of the South was the picture of Jesus praying in Gethsemane. Ironically, the President had died while sitting for a portrait at the Little White House in Warm Springs. *The Unfinished Portrait*, it would be named. And in the gloom after his death, on the slow train crawl through Georgia, up to Washington, D.C., America also seemed unfinished. Like Moses, Roosevelt had led his people out of the wilderness of despair and, like Moses, he would die too soon, too soon.

But the war that seemed to scorch the globe was ending even as a nation mourned.

On April 30, 1945, eighteen days after the President's death, the madman, Adolf Hitler, killed himself in a place called the Führerbunker in Berlin.

In August, A-bombs fell on Hiroshima and Nagasaki.

And then the war was over and the soldiers and sailors and war workers came home, and a kind of jubilation (or maybe it was a sigh, singing relief) hummed across the land. I was seven the year the war ended, a blurred-memory age. I have a dreamy sense of celebration, like spying on an adult party where glad-faced people preened with glad-faced smiles and behaved in a way that a child could not understand, but felt good about anyway.

The soldiers and sailors and war workers had stories and memories and ideas. They knew a thing or two about bravery. And tyranny. They knew a lot about tyranny. They weren't so easily bought by old promises of charge accounts at the fertilizer and feed store. No sir. They'd played that game. Or their parents had. And if they were old enough to fight, they had suffered the Great Depression first-hand, knew too well how long that belly-gnawing bad time had lingered. Enough was enough. They had the G.I. Bill and maybe some trade they'd picked up in the war–mechanics, welding, cooking. It didn't take them long to assess their options. Going back to the ass-end of a mule on someone else's place gradually gave way to getting on with their lives.

It was the true beginning of the thing called decentralization, especially for the sharecropper. Poetically, I think of it as an exodus of slow-moving people–farm to town, town to city, one state to another, generation following generation, leaving behind gravestones that carry the codes of a personal, yet dim, history.

I have always been intrigued with that period of time–the post-war years. Two of my novels are set in that period. I was at the right age, in the right place, for developing memories that are still clear and certain, and the clearest, most certain sensation from that period is the opposite of decentralization. It has to do with belonging to the units of a place and a family, of having boundaries.

In my first novel, *The Year the Lights Came On*, I wrote about it, and offer here an excerpt to describe it as I first realized it:

The Great Depression and World War Number Two had been our only experience with the Larger World, and we had inherited–through some curious process of osmosis–a possessed sense of belonging. Belonging was our constant defense, our way of warding off the suspected Great End. The Larger World had issued messages that we lived in a temporary time, that we, ourselves, were temporary. (The atomic bomb was one thing; now, in 1947, there was rumor about a bomb of such unpredictable destruction that certain international scientists were afraid it would create a molecular reaction and Earth would disintegrate in a series of explosions, like a string of Chinese firecrackers.)

Because of the Larger World, and what it said to us in the voices of the Radio Evening News Network and eight-point type of *The Anderson Independent*, we had been mightily influenced and had adopted the habit of clustering, as though clustering was an affirmation of our existence: if we saw one another, spoke with one another, then it must be true–we had survived.

In clustering, we became isolationists; in isolation, we assumed identities; in identity, we were assigned value; in value, we learned of imperatives; and, in imperatives, we realized perspective.

To the members of Our Side, perspective was conditioned by boundaries. Boundaries gave us reach, held us, dared us; boundaries tutored us in the deeper significance of belonging.

Wesley and I lived by the boundaries of Black Pool Swamp, circling us in a horseshoe from the south and east and west. To the north we were somehow contained by Banner's Crossing and Rakestraw Bridge Road.

There was a sense of being centrifugally leashed to the center of our north and south, east and west boundaries; the center was Home and Home would spin us out, but only to the invisible, protective edges of where we wandered, and then Home would draw us back again.

We could not mark those boundaries by stake and flag. They were not taught by a line drawn in shoe-edge, or plotted on some map from the Official Office of Official Boundaries. Our boundaries were established by instinct. We knew. We simply knew. We could chase after laughter and echoes of laughter until we were exhausted with exhilaration, and we could wander farther and farther away, safe, protected, until that one step–that one step too far, too threatening–and then we would retreat. No one told us to return. We knew. We simply knew. We knew when we had ventured too far, as though our sense of equilibrium had been savagely attacked.

But the Highway 17 Gang did not understand about boundaries. Highway 17 was alive with people moving, going great distances, and once having passed, whizzing in their automobiles, they were not likely to return that way again. The Highway 17 Gang watched those passing people and believed directions–north and south, east and west–were gray concrete roads drawn in heavy lines on service station maps.

The Highway 17 Gang did not have boundaries. They had yards. Somehow, they believed they were blessed.

When I wrote those words, in the early '70s, I had recently experienced the death of my mother, and a yearning for my youth–for the joy of those sparkling discoveries of the child-who-once-was–had become an unshakable obsession. I wanted to be the child again. From my fingertips, striking the words, the child returned. Magically, he returned. North and south, east and west, the child again roamed the boundaries of his boyhood, protected from the flood of change that would erode everything except memory.

But the writing of books is often as much an illusion as the magician's trick.

I think now that the Highway 17 Gang was better prepared for change than Our Side. They understood the meaning of *people moving, going great distances.*

A great distance for us–Our Side, the dirt-road farm youngsters–was a Saturday afternoon trip to Royston, a hard-earned quarter allowance in our pocket, and a system for spending it: nine cents for admission to The Royce Theater, a penny left for a penny pack of Kits. Best buy for the money anywhere. If you weren't piggish with them, a penny pack of Kits could last through a cowboy movie and a serial (*The Phantom*, or *Batman and Robin*, or *The Green Arrow*, or someone else equally remarkable). After the movie, maybe an ice cream cone from Wray's Drug Store, with a nickel or dime left for the collection plate on Sunday.

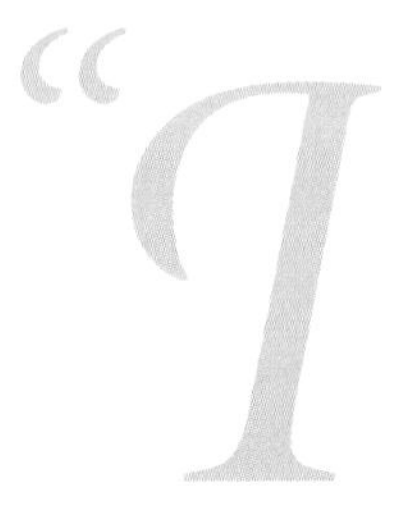

***wanted to be the child again. From my fingertips, striking the words, the child returned. Magically, he returned.*** ”

A Saturday afternoon in Royston was familiar adventure. Going to Elberton, or Hartwell, or Athens, was almost unimaginable. You might as well set your sights on Atlanta, or Miami, Florida, or New York City, New York. Elberton and Hartwell and Athens were miles away, and if you ever got there you never really felt good about it. All those strangers looking at you, funny-like, wondering who you were and why you were in their town, and if you had ever listened to rumor, you knew there were plenty of reasons to beware of such places. You couldn't expect a bargain in Elberton or Hartwell, even if they were advertising one with a carnival barker and a clown, and in Athens there was the University of Georgia, which turned normal people arrogant and sometimes rowdy. In Athens–the older boys vowed with wide-mouthed grins–there was a famous brothel. Everyone knew someone who had been there, or bragged that they had. If you had a lick of sense, you stayed in Royston. Royston was good enough. Everything a person could want could be found in Royston.

I think of those years fondly, as the best years, years of my Age of Innocence, before innocence gave way to experience, before I began my own exodus.

We bobbed along with the times, like fishing corks on a two-acre fish pond. On the surface, all seemed peaceful and serene, but things were roiling down where the fish lived. Odd things. Funny things. Frightening things.

In Roswell, New Mexico, a flying saucer supposedly malfunctioned and crashed to Earth, leaving little human-like creatures scattered over the ground.

Jackie Robinson, born in a Georgia sharecropper's house, showed up in a Brooklyn Dodgers uniform, the first black man to play baseball in the white man's major leagues, and in Royston, hometown of the great Ty Cobb, tongues clucked in disbelief.

In Walton County, four black people were assassinated, but the details were pretty much hushed up.

The Dead Sea Scrolls were discovered in Wadi Qumran, and revivalists bellowed "Amen!" over more hard proof of what they had been preaching.

Henry Ford, who gave us the automobile from the assembly line, died in 1947. So did Al Capone, who gave us crime to remember.

Joe Louis, the great Brown Bomber, was still heavyweight cham-peen of the world.

An electronic brain was put together at the University of Pennsylvania and people grinned at such nonsense and muttered, "Wonder what they're going to do with that?"

A United States airplane flew at supersonic speeds, as if getting some place was more important than the pleasure of the trip.

Everything was moving so fast that it made your head spin if you tried to take it all in at one sitting.

Yet, safe within our boundaries, little of it mattered, more than talk. Some of it even seemed senseless–a doctor named Benjamin Spock writing about raising children. My mother had given birth to eleven children at home, one in the hospital. What could this Dr. Spock teach her?

In Vanna, the community of my childhood, we crept along cautiously, following the philosophy my father once recited as advice: "Be not the first by which the new is tried, nor yet the last to lay the old aside."

In summer, the canning plant operated on the grounds of Vanna Junior High School, where crowds of women and children gathered to shell peas, snap beans, peel peaches, and to talk of how things were among the people they knew.

Dennis Harris, who sold Watkins products, still drove the backroads with his goods stuffed in his vehicle, bringing the aroma of vanilla and spices to linger invitingly in the heavy, hot air.

We still fished Beaverdam Creek for catfish, still raided watermelon patches, still played pasture baseball and football, still had our petty, temper-triggered fights, still smoked rabbit tobacco, still took our walks to Royston, still wondered about the carryings-on of people in such faraway places as Elberton and Hartwell and Athens.

And then, in 1947, electricity came to the farm families of Vanna, and nothing was the same.

In the fields, my brothers and sisters and I were singing "Zip-a-dee-doo-dah," "Shoo-Fly Pie and Apple Pan Dowdy," and "Doin' What Comes Nacherly." Dancing kind of songs. Loose-limbed kind of songs. We had electricity and an indoor toilet, a wringer washing machine on the back porch, vegetables in the garden, meat on the hoof, a Sears and Roebuck catalog to order from, if we couldn't find what we wanted at Gallant Belk, or Thornton's, or Blumenthal's, or one of the other enterprises located in Royston.

We were giving way, all right. Yessiree. Giving way to good times after bad.

*Zip-a-dee-doo-dah, zip-a-dee-a. Me, oh my, what a wonderful day ...*

That is how we lived.

*"If the house could talk, I would ask it to tell me stories of the night-whispering that must have taken place among the Careys and the Cromers and the Harts and the Carters and the Humans and the Crafts."*

But we were not sharecroppers.

We owned our farm and our home.

The Careys did not. They were tenants, sharecroppers.

Every bale of cotton we picked was ours. Every bale of cotton the Careys picked was only partly theirs. The rest they surrendered to the landlord. The same with corn and wheat and oats.

I do not remember ever hearing the Careys singing in the fields. Maybe they did. I simply don't remember it.

I think the Careys, like all tenant farmers, were balanced between giving way and giving up.

If the house could talk, I would ask it to tell me stories of the night-whispering that must have taken place among the Careys and the Cromers and the Harts and the Carters and the Humans and the Crafts.

But the house has lost its words, and in its silence, I can only invent.

> *"Don't know what we're going to do."*
>
> *"Look for a second job somewhere."*
>
> *"Doing what?"*
>
> *"Whatever's out there."*
>
> *"God help us."*
>
> *"If He's planning on it, He's taking his own sweet time getting around to it."*
>
> *"Don't talk about God like that."*
>
> *"Next time He plows a round for me, I'll tell Him I'm sorry."*

I know there was talk. Had to be.

Sometimes the words did slip out.

I remember a conversation between two sharecroppers at the Vanna Cotton Gin, two men old before their time, smoking finger-rolled cigarettes from Prince Albert tins, two men lamenting the boll weevil and the dry weather and the short staple of the cotton packed in their wagons and the bill at the store.

One of them said, "We ain't much better off than niggers."

The other wagged his head in agreement.

Today, much would be made of the comment. It would be called racist and mean-spirited. Critics would put a spin on it by talking indignantly about the N-word.

And they would be so wrong, so very wrong.

It wasn't a racist comment, not even mean-spirited. It was merely a point of reference, a hard and despairing truth. Class-to-class reality. The white sharecropper's family lived, in many ways, exactly like the black sharecropper's family. Being not *much better off* simply ackowledged that blacks were treated even worse– Colored Only water fountains, sitting in the balcony of The Royce Theater, buying from the side door at Wray's, getting the throw-away meat at hog killings.

In college, I would read clinically cold studies from those sociologists who were examining the nature of decentralization–studies where every sort of human behavior and condition could be explained to some degree of satisfaction by the clever use of theory and conclusion–and it occurred to me that, again and again, the sociologists were pointing their scholarly fingers at the word *economics* and fixing the blame. The economics of the South created sharecropping, they declared, just as it had created slavery.

They were right, of course–those sociologists, with their theories and conclusions. It was a matter of economics. There were those who had and those who didn't have, which seems to me to be the bottom line of human history. Haves and have-nots. The only thing left out of the conclusions of the sociologists was a sense of the drudgery of life suffered by the have-nots. Yet, it is not a deliberate omission. Only those who lived it could understand what it meant to be not much better off than anyone else.

That is why I would like to hear the stories of the house.

I am not interested in the economics of the people who lived there.

I would like to know about the trembling moments–the uncertainties, the fears, the anger, the rage, the bullying, the begging.

I want to hear the prayers that were offered up to God-beyond-the-ceiling-and-roof.

I want to hear the voices of sometimes-joy.

I want to know what caused the joy.

I want to know how the giving way took place.

It would be a story worth writing.

TERRY KAY

*Athens, Georgia*

# Catalogue of the Exhibition

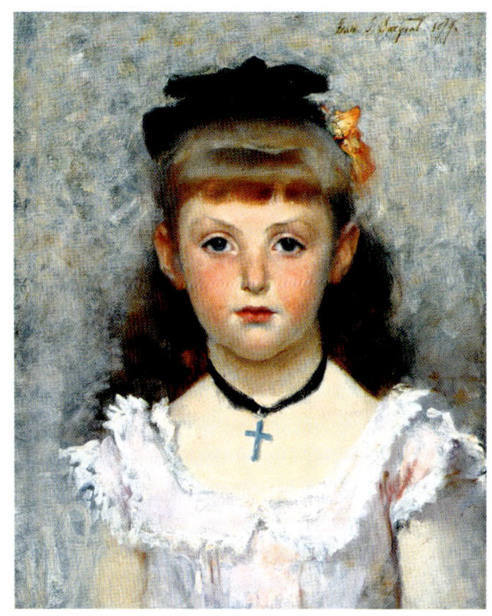

No. 40

# Artist Unknown

In the first half of the nineteenth century, itinerant portraitists dominated the art market in the South. The plantation owners' growing financial prosperity gave them the means and desire to memorialize in paint the social and economic status of their families. Portraits like the present example were painted by artists who traveled throughout the South garnering commissions from eager patrons. They generally derived their compositions from European prototypes, notably through prints, which had guided American painters for a century. Beginning in the 1820s, a number of French-born and -trained artists set up studios in New Orleans and traveled throughout the South. They executed portraits characterized by sharp realism and precise draftsmanship. This concern for careful drawing is evident in the portrait of Susan Holmes Taylor, in which the meticulously drawn facial features and detailed, multi-layered dress of the young girl suggest that the artist may have been exposed to the French academic tradition. The English travel writer Frances Trollope wrote of the American view of portraiture: "From all the conversations which I listened to in America, I found that the finish of drapery was considered as the highest excellence, and next to this, the resemblance in a portrait; I do not remember ever to have heard the words drawing or composition used in any conversation on the subject." [1]

While the art of portraiture was becoming increasingly bourgeois in character, the prosperous land-owning gentry continued to be portraitists' greatest patrons. Such is the case with the painting of Susan Holmes Taylor (1854-1901), who is shown seated on the extensive grounds of her family home in Athens, Georgia. In contrast to the earlier southern vogue for miniatures, the size of this composition was appropriate for the large, formal parlor of a plantation home and bespoke her wealth and high social status. Anecdotal records indicate that the portrait was executed at the Taylor-Grady house, still standing near downtown Athens, built by Susan's grandfather, General Robert Taylor, in 1845. Much in the tradition of colonial portraiture, the young girl is painted as a "small adult," with a reserve and restraint foreign to a child her age. One can see, however, that the artist attempted, albeit unsuccessfully, to represent the more impetuous nature of childhood. Flowers, symbolically associated with fertility and femininity, spill from her lap as an indication of her youthful restlessness. Her childish pose is visually outweighed by her steadfast gaze and delicate, if somewhat awkwardly drawn, arms which curve into her lap.

---

1 Information taken from Bruce W. Chambers, *Art and Artists of the South* (Columbia: University of South Carolina Press, 1984); and Jessie Poesch, *The Art of the Old South: Painting, Sculpture, Architecture and the Products of Craftsmen, 1560-1860* (New York: Alfred A. Knopf, 1983).

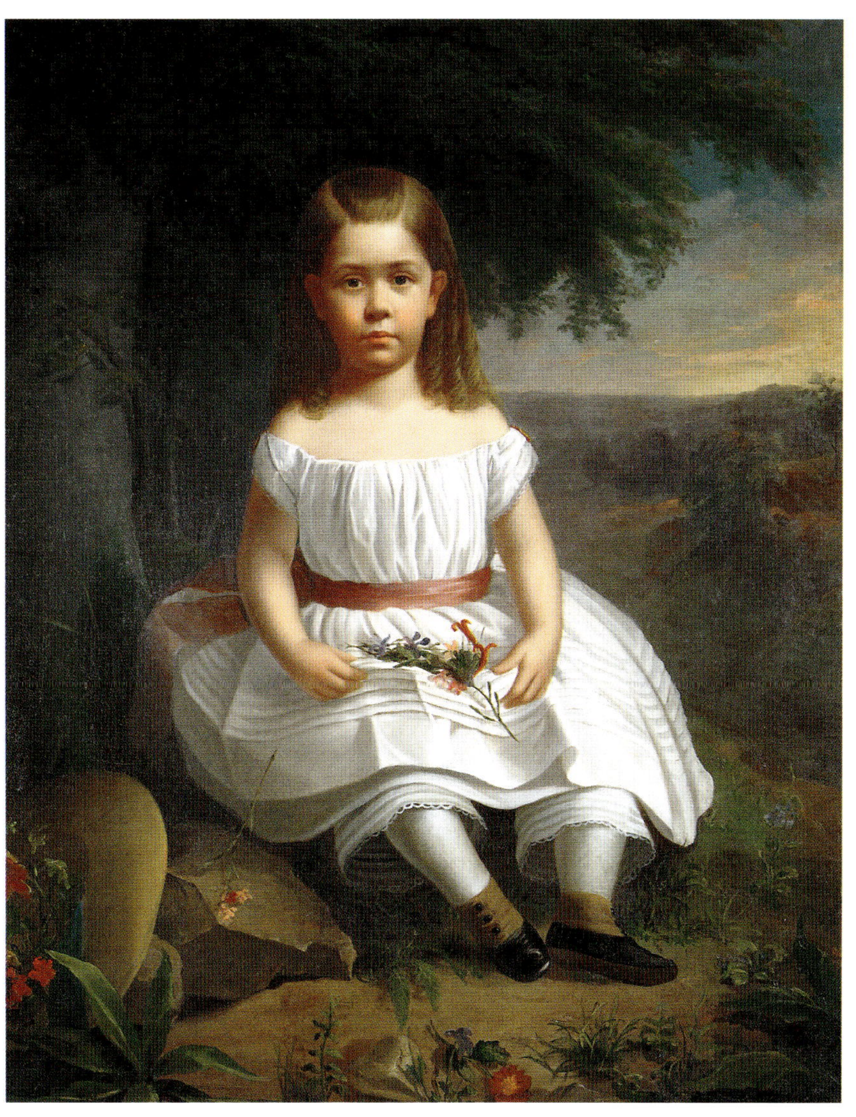

**No. 1**

ARTIST UNKNOWN
*Susan Holmes Taylor,* 1858
Oil on canvas
40 x 32 inches
Private collection

# Lamar Baker

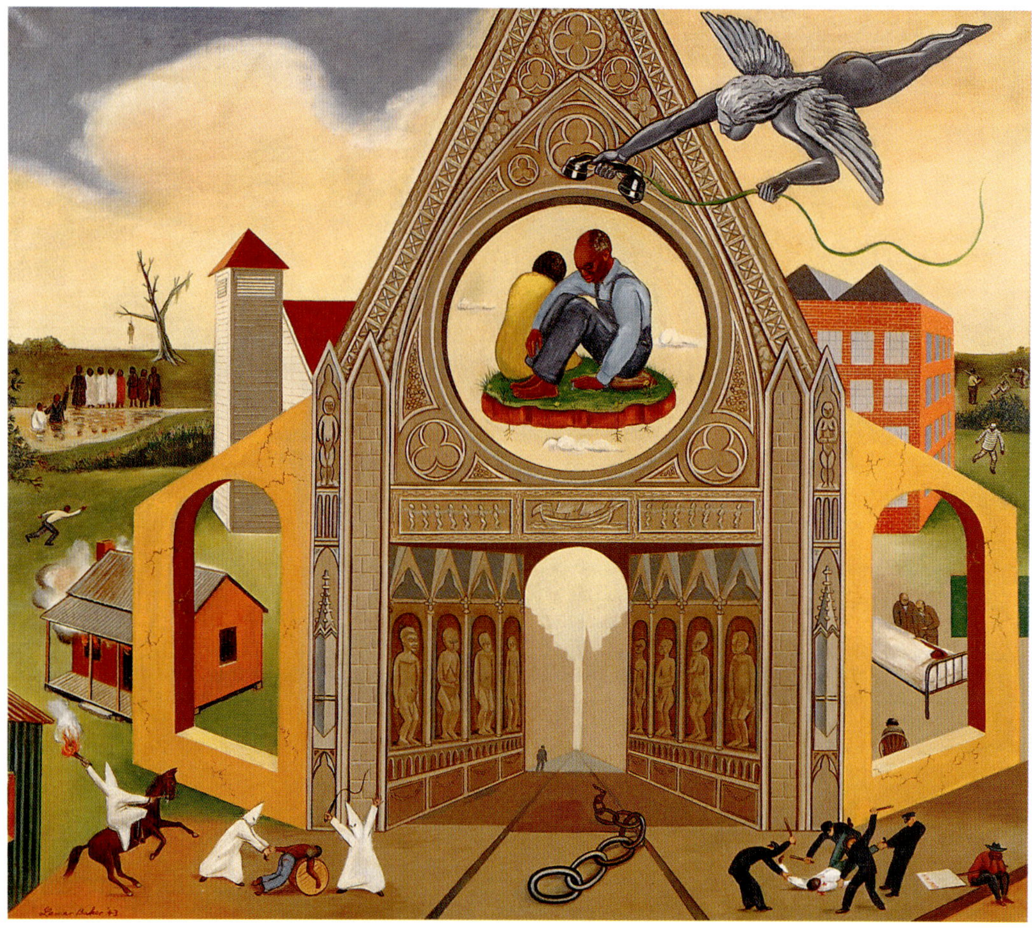

No. 2

Lamar Baker (American, 1908-1994)
*Nobody Knows the Trouble I've Seen but Jesus (Negro Spiritual #1)*, 1943
Oil and tempera on canvas
36 x 42 inches
Collection of the Columbus Museum, Columbus, Georgia

Lamar Baker began his artistic training at the Sketch Club and the Art School of the High Museum in his hometown of Atlanta, Georgia. After graduating from the University of Georgia in 1935, Baker continued his studies at the Art Students League in New York under painter Kenneth Hayes Miller and printmaker Harry Sternberg. Regionalism and Social Realism dominated American art during the 1930s, and Baker was exposed to both major movements during his five years in New York. John Steuart Curry, Grant Wood, and Thomas Hart Benton depicted the American scene, but unlike Baker, these Regionalist artists focused on the Midwest, the so-called heartland of America, and painted nostalgic rural scenes. The politically motivated art of the Social Realists portrayed the urban poor and working classes using a style influenced by the work of Robert Henri. The Social Realists often worked for magazines, including *The Masses*, a well-known Socialist publication whose contributors included John Sloan and George Bellows. Baker's art also incorporated Surrealist fantasy, which was gaining in popularity in the 1930s. Baker combined the regional characteristics of his southern upbringing with a concern for the racial and economic inequalities plaguing the region. He returned to Atlanta in 1951 to pursue his career in art. The next year, he moved to Columbus, Georgia, where he worked as a designer and draftsman for the Litho-Krome Company. As a white southerner, Baker provided an original commentary on the African-American experience in the South, one which separates his work from nearly all of his contemporaries working in the region.[1]

In 1942, Baker received the prestigious Julius Rosenwald Fellowship, which funded a trip to Louisiana and Mississippi. During his travels, he developed an idea for a series of five paintings that focused on traditional African-American spirituals. *Nobody Knows the Trouble I've Seen but Jesus (Negro Spiritual #1)* is the first in the series and presents a surrealistic scene of the persecution of blacks. A landscape dominated by a church facade provides the setting for a series of disturbing vignettes recounting one man's struggle to survive. The central, circular window frames an older man perched on a small plot of grass floating in heaven. Freed from the chain below, he gazes down at his past. His baptism in the rural South, depicted in the upper-left corner of the composition, is set against an eerie backdrop of a lynching scene. The man is portrayed as a victim of blatant persecution by both the Ku Klux Klan and the police. This equation of a self-proclaimed organization of bigots with a governmental agency sworn to protect was a reality for many in the rural South. Salvation is provided in the form of a telephone call from Jesus, whose presence is implied by the angelic apparition in the sky.

1 Biographical information taken from: Patricia Phagan, ed., *The American Scene and the South: Paintings and Works on Paper, 1930-1946*, Exhib. cat. (Athens: Georgia Museum of Art, 1996).

# Louis Betts

Louis Betts, born in Little Rock, Arkansas, was one of several artists in his family. While he received instruction from his father, the landscape painter Edwin Daniel Betts, Sr., his training at the Pennsylvania Academy of the Fine Arts under William Merritt Chase encouraged him to develop an impressionistic aesthetic. He made the first of many trips to Europe on an art scholarship and returned to the States with an increased interest in Impressionism. Betts enjoyed commercial success as a portrait painter and worked throughout his career in Chicago, New York, London, Paris, Amsterdam, and Madrid. He was elected an associate member of the National Academy of Design in 1912 and became a full member three years later.[1] Critical acclaim soon followed. A critic with *International Studio* noted, "His grasp of character and essentials is revealed in a broad and dashing manner . . . . He is a painter's painter in the truest meaning whose work will ever appeal to connoisseurs."[2]

*The Yellow Parasol* is one in a series executed during Betts's stay at the famous Impressionist artists' colony in Old Lyme, Connecticut. Even though Old Lyme was crowded with artists, which caused the center's creativity to diminish by the 1920s, works like *The Yellow Parasol* demonstrate the power of the landscape to inspire paintings of sun-drenched garden scenes, a popular motif of American Impressionist painters, notably Frederick Carl Frieseke.[3] Betts's bright palette and broken brushstrokes pay tribute to his teacher Childe Hassam, who by this time had distanced himself from the colony. As Estill Curtis Pennington notes in *A Southern Collection*, the rather decorative figures cloaked in costumes of the Colonial Revival look to the past "even as the noise of jazz-age cubism was nearly deafening."[4] Indeed, the 1920s witnessed a broad revival of interest in the country's colonial past as demonstrated by the reconstruction of Colonial Williamsburg. The critical success of the painting, evidenced by its award-winning debut at the National Academy of Design in 1925, points to America's desire for art that in subject matter and style returned the country to time-worn traditions.

---

1 Biographical information taken from Helen L. Earle, *Biographical Sketches of American Artists*, 5th ed. (Collingswood: Anthony C. Schmidt Fine Arts, 1972), 44; and Estill Curtis Pennington, *A Southern Collection* (Augusta: Morris Communications Corporation, 1992), 110.

2 Earle, 44.

3 William Gerdts, *American Impressionism* (New York: Artabras Publishers, 1984), 227.

4 Pennington, 110.

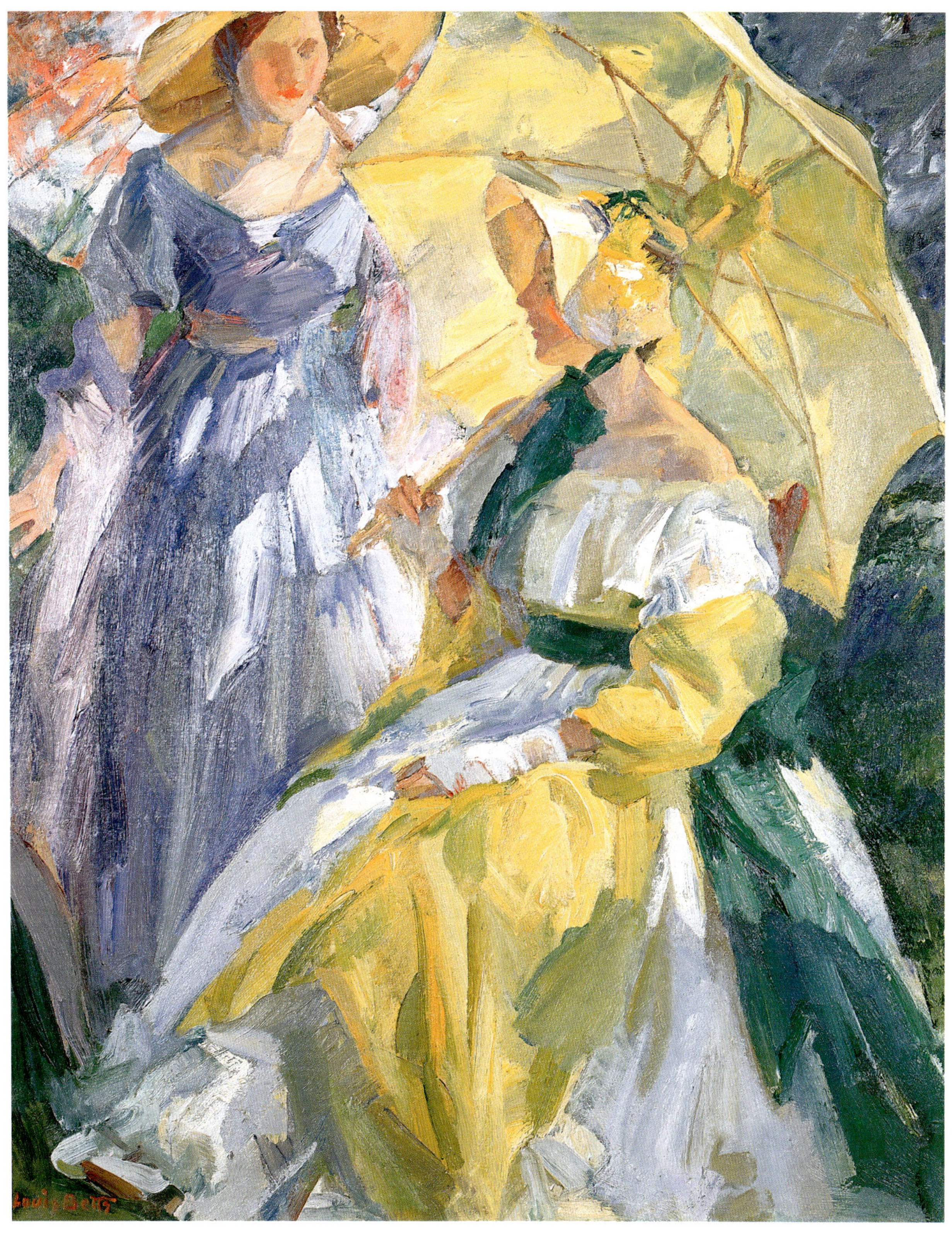


~ **No. 3** ~

Louis Betts (American, 1873-1961), *The Yellow Parasol*, ca. 1925.
Oil on canvas, 50 x 40 inches. Morris Museum of Art, Augusta, Georgia.

# Ralph Albert Blakelock

RALPH ALBERT BLAKELOCK, the son of a homeopathic physician, spent the first thirty years of his life in New York. He lived for a time with James Johnson, a musician friend of the family, who encouraged the young artist's talents. In 1864, Blakelock entered the Free Academy, later renamed the City College, but quit after two years to pursue a career in art. After the Civil War, many artists employed by the government traveled west to document the newly opened territories; however, when Blakelock departed in 1869, he did so as an independent artist. Blakelock sketched the Native Americans, wildlife, and spectacular scenery but never alluded to the growing industrial and urban presence in the West. He returned to New York via Mexico, Panama, and Jamaica. Blakelock spent the next twenty years transforming his memories of the West into poetic depictions of Indian encampments. Much in the spirit of his contemporaries, Albert Pinkham Ryder and George Inness, Blakelock's intimate and atmospheric depictions evoke more nostalgia than the reality of the West. Animals and humans float through the dense paint like spirits called from the dead. The dark forest interiors indicate no particular location, and by 1880, Blakelock had transformed the West's vast, sublime tracts into a place of mystery and wonder. He lent the same emotive qualities to his lesser-known cityscapes, seascapes, and still lifes, which like his landscapes reworked specific compositional patterns while varying the color scheme and surface density. During the years between his return to New York in 1872 and his final confinement in a mental institution in 1899, Blakelock's visionary and symbolist art was highly praised and exhibited at all the important venues of the day. The pressure to support his large family led to his initial breakdown in 1891, from which he never fully recovered. Hospitalized in Middletown, New York, Blakelock continued to create intimate landscapes, although he never profited from their sale. His notorious guardian, Mrs. Van Rensselaer Adams, who assumed control over the Blakelock estate, swindled the artist and his family out of their rightful inheritance. The tragedy surrounding Blakelock's demise was exacerbated by the numerous dealers and galleries who were in the lucrative business of producing Blakelock forgeries. As the artist rarely signed or dated his works, the market is still flooded with counterfeits.[1]

Paintings like *Night Moon*, identified by the Nebraska Blakelock Inventory at the University of Nebraska as by the artist's hand, separate themselves from forgeries by the unmistakable craftsmanship unique to Blakelock's work. The thick layers of pigment, varnish, and glaze reflect and absorb light and

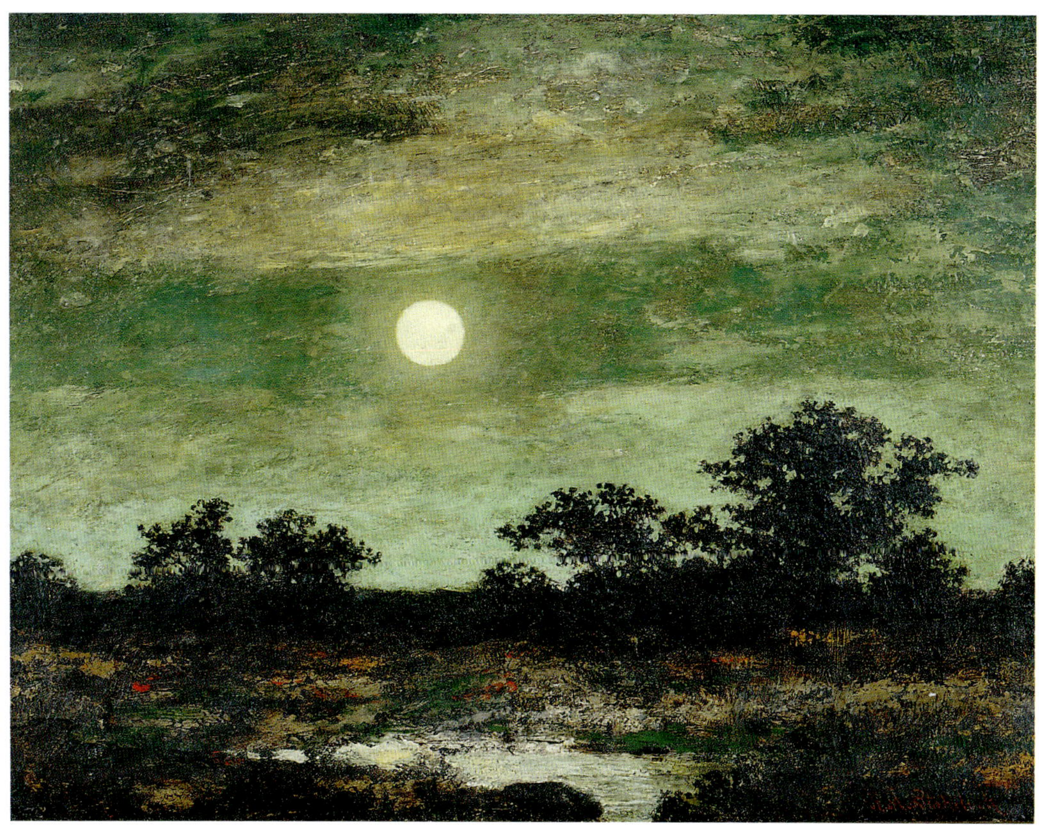

**No. 4**

Ralph Albert Blakelock (American, 1845-1919)
*Night Moon*
Oil on canvas
13 ½ x 17 ½ inches
Collection of Terry and Margaret Stent

create an image informed more by mood than by a particular style of drawing or modeling of forms. The moon-drenched foreground reveals what Norman Geske, director of the Blakelock Inventory, refers to as the "growth processes of vegetation." The delicate and individual textures of the grasses, rocks, and water, illuminated by the moon, demonstrate Blakelock's poetic understanding of the great variety in nature's bounty.

---

1 Biographical material taken from Abraham A. Davidson, *Ralph Albert Blakelock* (University Park: The Pennsylvania State University Press, 1987); Dorinda Evans, "Art and Deception: Ralph Blakelock and His Guardian," *The American Art Journal* 19 (1987): 39-48; and Norman Geske, *Ralph Albert Blakelock, 1849-1919*, Exhib. cat. (Lincoln: Sheldon Memorial Art Gallery, 1975).

# John Bunyan Bristol

JOHN BUNYAN BRISTOL WAS BORN in Hillsdale, New York. With the exception of a few lessons from portrait painter Henry Ary, he was largely a self-taught artist.[1] Nevertheless, by 1858 he was a regular exhibitor at the National Academy of Design and became a member in 1875.[2] Bristol established residence in New York but spent most summers working in New England, where the mountains and lakes provided inspiration and subject matter for his landscapes. Traveling extensively along the eastern seaboard, he produced tropical landscapes of Florida early in his career, but later he focused almost exclusively on the northern regions of the United States.[3] Bristol executed these commercially popular rural landscapes with a naturalism free of idealism.

The Berkshire Mountains were a favorite theme for Bristol. *Landscape, Monument Mountain from the Berkshire Meadow* is an excellent example of the artist's concern with natural light and realistic detail. Much like his predecessors John Frederick Kensett and Asher B. Durand, Bristol brought together land and water within his compositions in order to demonstrate the fecundity of the American landscape. Suggested by the campsite along the river and the hint of a church tower in the distance, man exists in harmony with nature, and completes the picturesque image of the Berkshire region. Bristol painted this picture shortly following the Civil War; at this time, the singularity of the northeastern landscape was being seriously challenged by the grandeur of the Rocky Mountains and California. Moreover, much of New England had lost its agrarian character as industry, an expanding population, and an extensive railway system rendered such views old-fashioned and nostalgic. Such visions of an Arcadia fixed within a traditional network of trees and mountains, bathed in a luminous light, and linked by meandering paths have their roots in the Hudson River school landscapes of the years leading up to the Civil War.

---

1 Michael David Zellman, *American Art Analog*, vol. 1 (New York: Chelsea House Publishers, 1986), 218.

2 George C. Groce and David H. Wallace, *The New-York Historical Society's Dictionary of Artists in America* (New Haven: Yale University Press, 1957), 82.

3 Biographical information taken from ibid., 82; and Zellman, 218.

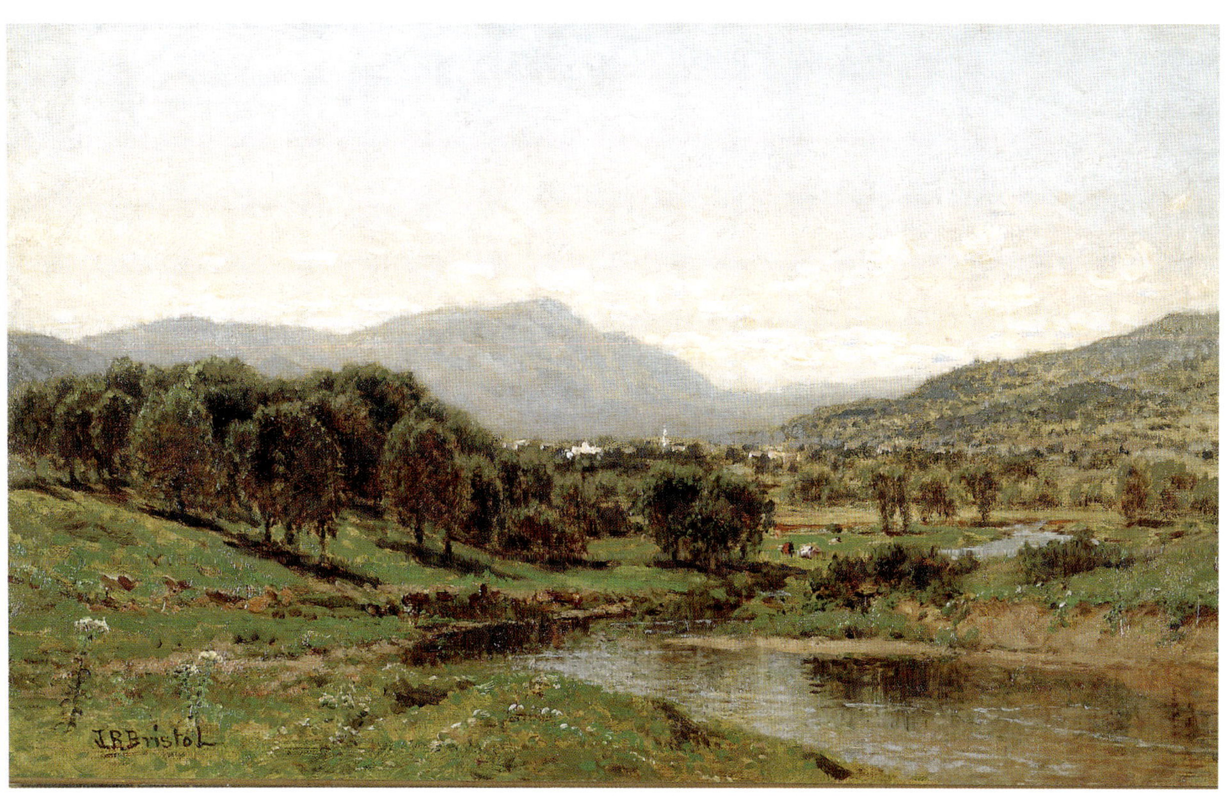


**No. 5**

JOHN BUNYAN BRISTOL (AMERICAN, 1826-1909)
*Landscape, Monument Mountain from the Berkshire Meadow*, ca. 1870
Oil on canvas
30 x 42 inches
Collection of Mr. and Mrs. David E. Miller, Jr.

# *Theodore Butler*

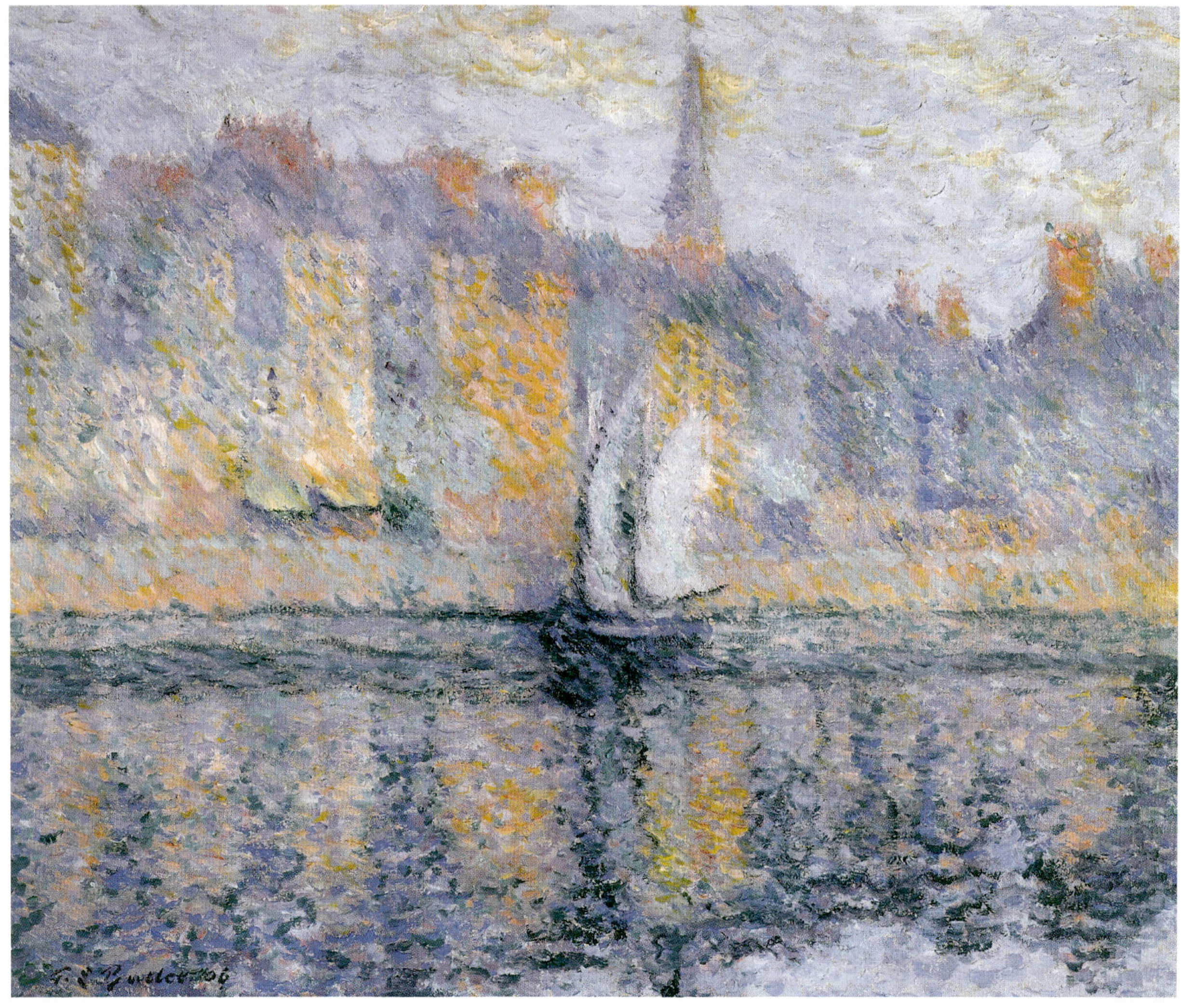

**No. 6**

THEODORE BUTLER (AMERICAN, 1861-1936)
*Honfleur*, 1906
Oil on canvas
22 ¼ x 27 ½ inches
Collection of Dr. and Mrs. Tom Cooper

THEODORE BUTLER GREW up in rural Ohio as the son of a successful businessman. His first real exposure to art came at age twenty-two, when Butler moved to New York to train at the Art Students League. Like his colleagues Philip Leslie Hale, Frank Duveneck, and William Merritt Chase, Butler painted with the dark realism of the popular Munich school style. In 1887, he traveled to Paris and briefly studied at the Académie Julian, the Académie Colarossi, and the Grande Chaumière. A year later, after receiving an honorable mention at the Paris Salon, Butler made his first trip to the new artists' colony in Giverny. Like so many artists who were slowly abandoning the darker palette of their early training, Butler began to adopt the Impressionist aesthetic. In 1892, he married Claude Monet's stepdaughter, Suzanne Hoschedé, and set up permanent residence in Giverny. After Butler's wife died in 1899, Marthe, her sister, helped raise the children and in the process developed a close relationship with him; they married a year later. Gradually, Butler's style departed from the aesthetic developed by Monet and took on the more robust qualities of the Post-Impressionist and Expressionist movements. The outbreak of World War I caused the Butlers' brief visit to America in 1913 to turn into a seven-year stay. During those years, Butler remained active, exhibiting at the Armory Show of 1913 and the Panama-Pacific Exhibition of 1915. In addition Butler, along with his friend John Sloan, was a founding member of the Independent Artists of America. In 1921, Butler returned to Giverny, where he continued to work until his death.[1]

*Honfleur* is one of a series of views Butler executed of the popular French fishing village and resort in the summer of 1906. This painting may have been exhibited as part of that series at the Société des Artistes Indépendants in Paris in 1907. Butler adopted the late Impressionist style of his father-in-law and Pierre Bonnard and Edouard Vuillard. Beginning with the observation of nature, in line with Impressionist practice, Butler, like his French contemporaries, broke the forms into abstract patterns of blues and pinks that separate the composition into horizontal bands. The harmony of the image is in marked contrast to the energetic and more expressionistic work of the contemporary Fauves, who caused such a stir at the Paris Salon of 1907.

1 Biographical material taken from William H. Gerdts, *Impressionism and Post-Impressionism: Transformations in the Modern Mode: 1885-1945* (New York: Grand Central Galleries, 1988); and Donald D. Keyes, *American Impressionism in Georgia Collections*, Exhib. cat. (Athens: Georgia Museum of Art, 1993), 20.

# *Mary Cassatt*

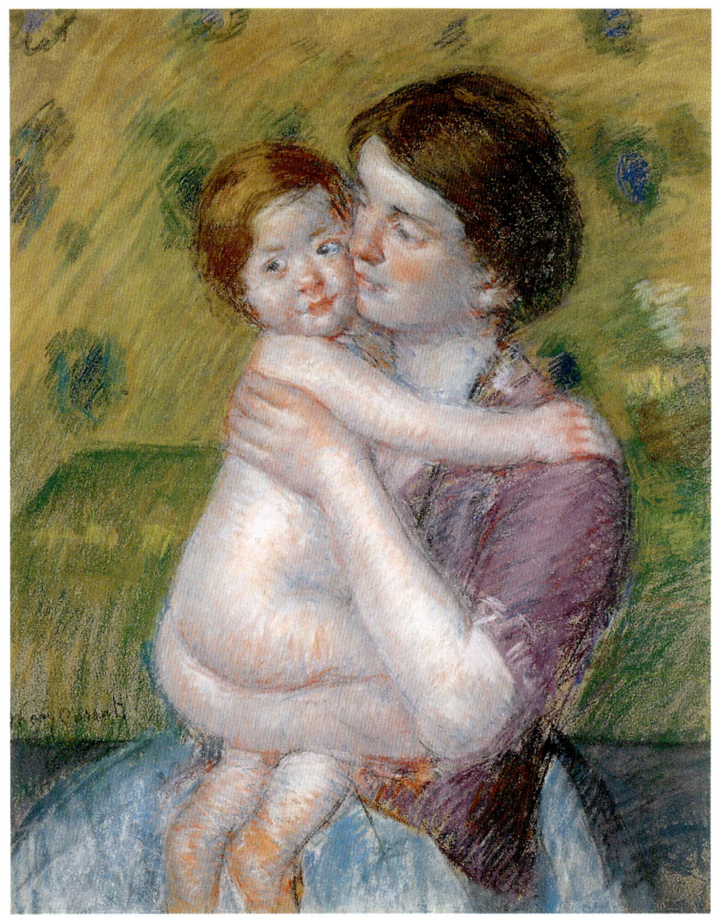

**No. 7**

MARY CASSATT (AMERICAN, 1844-1926)
*Mother and Child*, ca. 1909-14
Pastel on canvas
39 ¾ x 26 ½ inches
Collection of Kathryn W. Hartzog

MARY STEVENSON Cassatt, born into a life of privilege, spent five of her first ten years in Europe with her family. Her father, a banker, returned with his wife and daughter to Pennsylvania in 1855 and promptly enrolled Mary in art classes at the Pennsylvania Academy of the Fine Arts. At twenty, she decided to pursue a career in art, and studied in France under the academic painter Jean-Léon Gérôme. Cassatt's real education, however, stemmed from her later friendships with the young radicals Edouard Manet and Edgar Degas. After briefly studying the work of the Old Masters in Italy and Spain, Cassatt settled in Paris in 1873. Encouraged by Degas, she entered the circle of French Impressionists, with whom she exhibited in 1879, 1880, 1881, and 1886.[1] Like her colleagues, Cassatt was fascinated by the contemporary scene and depicted the transitory moments of life with a freshness and spontaneity foreign in academic circles. She employed a free brushstroke and became increasingly interested in color. Her financial independence allowed her to experiment without fear of commercial failure. Cassatt's variations on the theme of domesticity came to dominate her later work, in part as a response to conservative criticism.[2]

Although Cassatt broke into the male-dominated art world, she felt no desire to paint the heroic public adventures of men. For Cassatt, the intimate, private, domestic world of women and their children was the female equivalent to Thomas Eakins's depictions of sporting outdoorsmen. Beginning in the late 1880s, Cassatt executed a large number of mother and child images in oils, pastels, and prints. She resisted completely cloaking her theme in Victorian sentimentality by keeping her subjects true to their human nature; thus, she modernized an ancient theme. In *Mother and Child*, the infant appears distracted, her eyes gazing beyond the picture plane. The mother holds the child near, placing one hand on the twisting child's back to stabilize her. By depicting this rather awkward moment, Cassatt broke from the conventional portraits of mother and child to portray an intimate, transitory instant in the sitters' lives. Enhanced by the new medium of pastel, their relationship is examined free of any distinct narrative, as Cassatt chose to define the background only sketchily and removed any peripheral objects from the composition.

*This work has been removed from the exhibition.*

---

1 Stephen F. Eisenman, *Nineteenth-Century Art: A Critical History* (London: Thames and Hudson, 1994), 255.

2 Biographical information taken from Gerdts, *American Impressionism*, and Nancy Mowll Mathews, *Mary Cassatt* (New York: Harry N. Abrams, Inc., 1997).

# George Cooke

THE ITINERANT PORTRAIT painter George Cooke was largely a self-taught artist. One of seven children raised in St. Mary's County, Maryland, Cooke relied on a sharp eye for imitation in his initial attempts at portrait painting. It remained, however, a recreational diversion until 1820, when his various occupations in the mercantile and land speculation businesses failed. Cooke spent the next few years traveling throughout Virginia and Alabama, where he painted portraits for friends and family. He received his first formal training from Charles Bird King at his gallery in Richmond, Virginia, and continued his studies in Europe. Cooke and his wife, Maria Ann Heath, traveled to Paris in 1826 and then to Florence, Rome, and Naples. He filled canvases and sketchbooks with copies of Old Master paintings and drawings from ancient statues and paintings. The American press praised his European efforts, examples of which hung in fellow artist Chester Harding's painting rooms, stating, "It is hoped that Mr. Cook's [*sic*] paintings may prove a happy exception to the general fate of American productions, and that he may receive that generous patronage which his talents so richly merit." Upon his return to America in 1830, Cooke was elected an academician of the American Academy of Fine Arts and an associate member of the National Academy of Design. He exhibited at both of these prestigious venues as well as at the Pennsylvania Academy of the Fine Arts and the Apollo Association in New York City. Cooke resumed his peripatetic existence in the 1840s, traveling throughout Georgia, Alabama, and Louisiana. He continued to fulfill portrait and landscape commissions, and in 1844, he announced plans to establish a "permanent gallery of painting" in New Orleans. Exhibitions featured the works of Thomas Cole, Thomas Doughty, Thomas Sully, Emanuel Leutze, and Daniel Huntington as well as Cooke's own works based on Old Master paintings. The financial failure of the gallery, coupled with Cooke's failing health, forced him into retirement in 1848. He died of Asiatic cholera a year later, and his once solid reputation faded into anonymity.[1]

Throughout his career, George Cooke often enjoyed the benevolence of prominent jurist Augustin Smith Clayton during extended visits to Athens, Georgia:

> ***Such hospitality I have scarcely ever seen, but the conduct of Mrs. [Augustin] Clayton, whose house has been our home for four months, overwhelms us with gratitude. She is the widow of the late Judge C. and [illegible] recently a member of Congress; left in***

> *affluence with her children all married except the two youngest daughters, aged 7 and 14, insists on our staying with her as company and protection–and being a devoted member of the Methodist church, she and Maria agree like two angels in all that is good. As she will not accept of board I have to make handsome presents to remove the Wright of Obligations, we are under.*[2]

As partial repayment for their kindness, Cooke executed a portrait of Mrs. Clayton's daughter-in-law, Leonora Harper Clayton, and two of her eleven children. Cooke's choice of an Italianate oval composition for his depiction of mother and children reflects the extensive time he spent in Europe copying the Old Masters. In addition, there had been an increasing interest in religious painting in the United States since the late eighteenth century. Cloaked in white, Leonora Harper Clayton is depicted as the chaste, moral guardian of domestic harmony. The two children present the viewer with flowers, demonstrating their civilized demeanor.

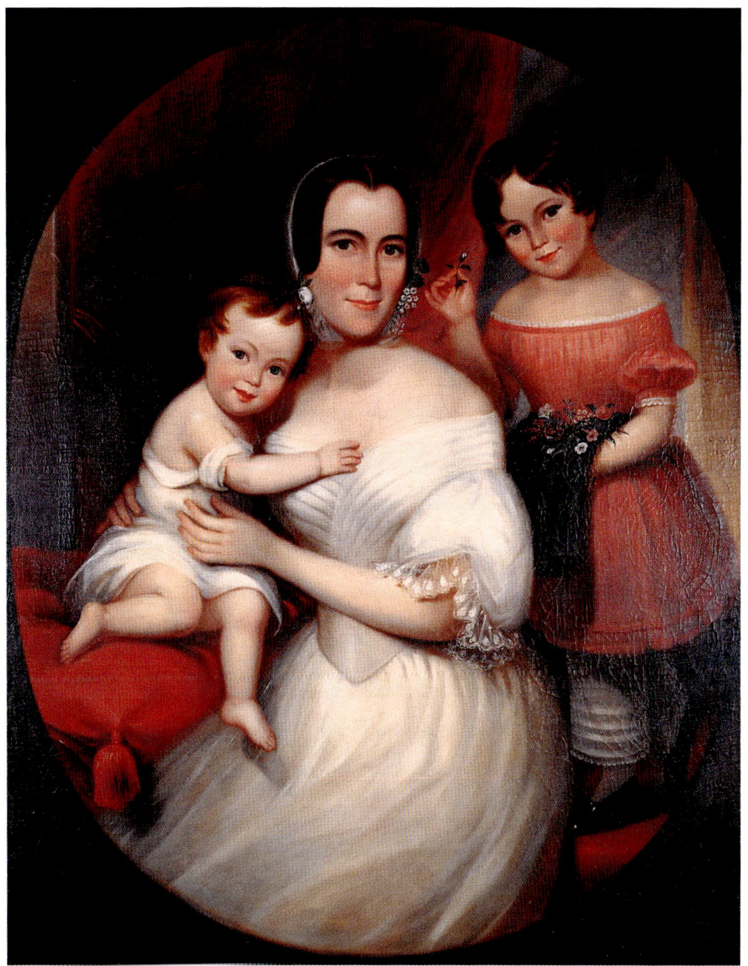

**No. 8**

GEORGE COOKE (AMERICAN, 1793-1849)
*Leonora Harper Clayton (Mrs. Philip A.) and Her Children, Philip and Julia Florence,* 1842
Oil on canvas
50 x 40 inches
Collection of Mary Ann Rogers Hammaker

---

1 Biographical information taken from Linda Crocker Simmons, "The Life of George Cooke," in *George Cooke 1793-1849*, Exhib. cat. (Athens: Georgia Museum of Art, 1991).

2 George Cooke to James Cooke, 6 February 1841 (MHS), quoted in ibid., 66.

# Colin Campbell Cooper

Colin Campbell Cooper is perhaps best known for his impressionistic renderings of New York. Born in Philadelphia, Cooper began his tutelage under the realist painter Thomas Eakins at the Pennsylvania Academy of the Fine Arts. Although he resided in Philadelphia until 1904 and eventually settled in New York, he lived a nomadic existence, constantly traveling between America and the Impressionist artists' colony in Giverny. In France, Cooper, as well as the other American Impressionists, learned the freedom of brushstroke and brightness of palette that had been used so successfully by the French Impressionists. Frustrated by the limitations of the more conventional academic schools, Cooper decried "too much stress on correctness of drawing and not enough on correctness of expression. Hard facts–bones and muscles in exactly the right place–are only the beginning–[and] will never make great pictures. They are only technical cornerstones." [1] Cooper utilized the *plein-air* technique of painting outdoors without preliminary sketching to give his works a freshness that he believed lacking in the more academic renderings of his contemporaries. In 1921, at the behest of Guy Rose, his colleague from Giverny, he went to California, where he completed his career working and teaching at the Stickney School in Pasadena.[2]

Cooper's fascination with crowded street scenes is demonstrated in his depiction of Wall Street in 1903. Businessmen, tourists, street vendors, and horse-drawn carriages jostle each other in the famous thoroughfare and at times blend into rusticated buildings and storefronts. The narrow composition is lined by towering skyscrapers that dwarf the human activity below, yet never pose the dark threat often depicted in similar cityscapes by contemporary realist Robert Henri. The edifices, soaring into the blue sky above, offer an optimistic, almost poetic view of urban life. Childe Hassam presented an equally celebratory view of American urban success in his patriotic *Flag* series, executed between 1916 and 1919. Both artists were likely influenced by Claude Monet's and Camille Pissaro's well-known impressionistic renderings of the narrow Parisian boulevards. Cooper stated in his article "Skyscrapers and How to Build them in Paint," published in *Palette and Bench* in 1909:

> *There is something in the sparkle of the thing, not only in the big masses of light and shade, but in the little details–which are like grace notes in a bar of music–that must be noted on the instant. There are infinite and subtle varieties of color in the windows of buildings where, at different angles, they take sky and cloud reflections.*[3]

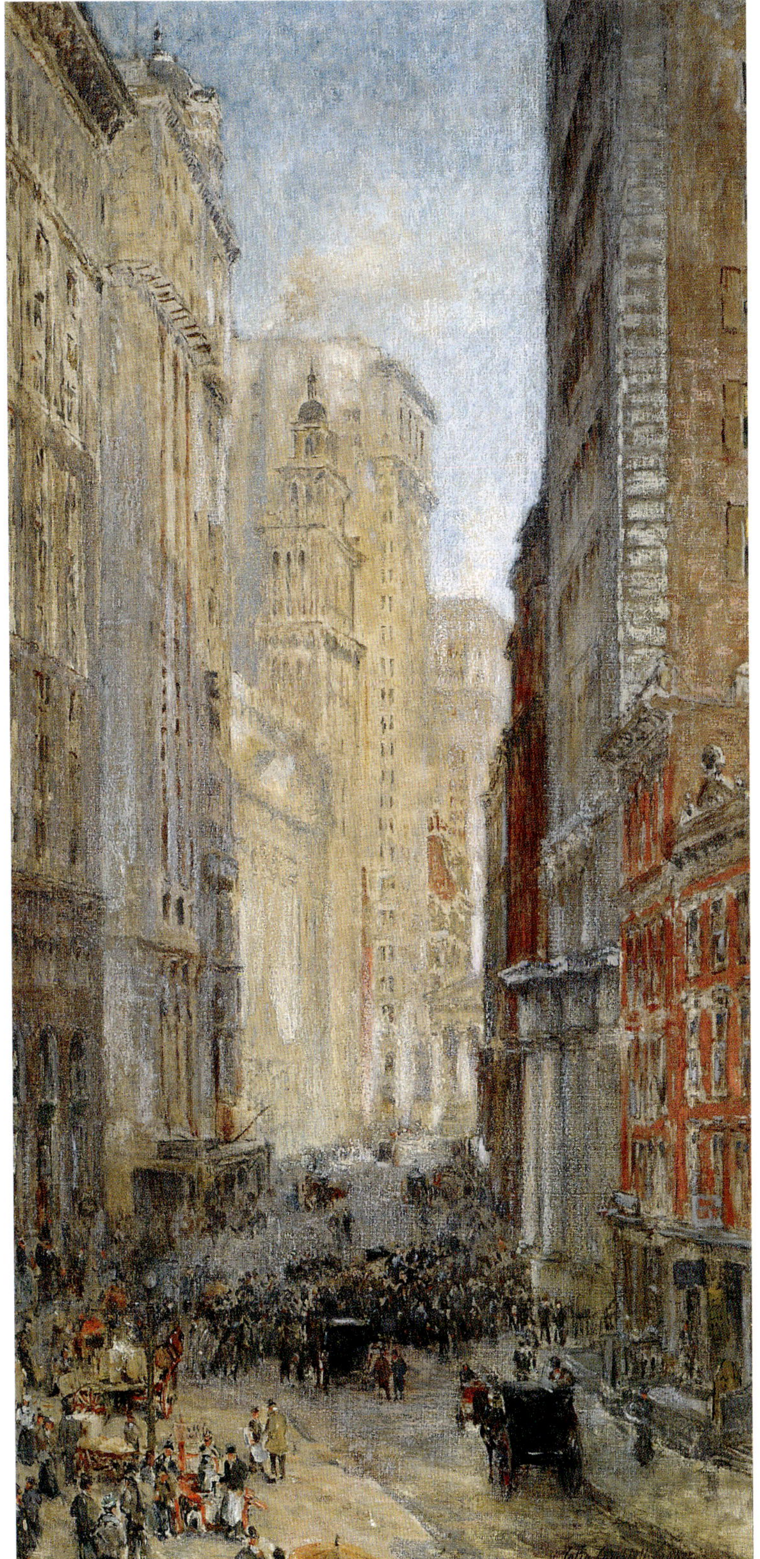

1 From an undated manuscript, Cooper File, Pennsylvania Academy of the Fine Arts, Archives of American Art, microfilm reel P73, quoted in William H. Gerdts, *Masterworks of American Impressionism from the Pfeil Collection* (Alexandria: Art Services International, 1992), 100.

2 Biographical information taken from ibid., 100; and Tina Goolsby, "Colin Campbell Cooper: An American Impressionist with a Global Perspective," *Art & Antiques* 6 (January-February 1983): 56-62.

3 Quoted in Doreen Bolger Burke, *American Paintings in the Metropolitan Museum of Art*, vol. 3 (New York: Metropolitan Museum of Art, 1980), n.p.

**No. 9**

COLIN CAMPBELL COOPER
(AMERICAN, 1856-1937)
*Wall Street*, 1903
Oil on canvas
40 x 20 inches
Collection of Terry and Margaret Stent

# Paul Cornoyer

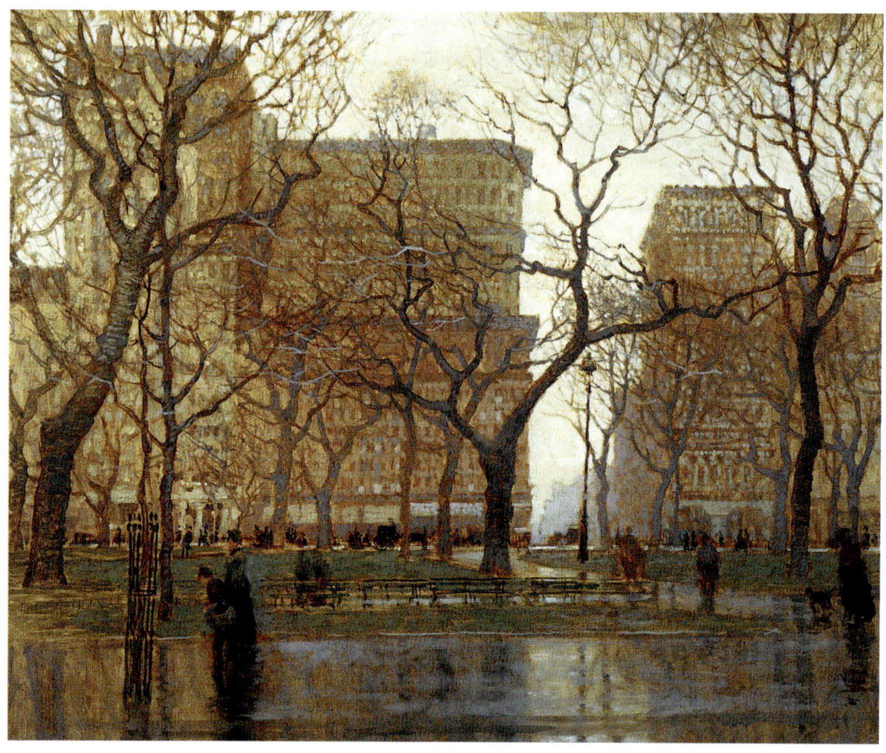

~ **No. 10** ~

Paul Cornoyer (American, 1864-1923)
*After the Rain,* ca. 1900
Oil on canvas
22 x 27 inches
Collection of Barbara Guillaume Griffin

Paul Cornoyer was born in St. Louis, Missouri, and attended the St. Louis School of Fine Arts. Like most post-Civil War artists, he traveled to Paris to study in 1879 under Jules-Joseph Lefebvre, Benjamin Constant, and Louis Blanc at the Académie Julian. Cornoyer remained in Paris for five years and returned to America in 1884. He received first prize from the prestigious American Artists Association in 1892 and a gold medal from the St. Louis Association of Painters and Sculptors. It would not be until the artist accepted a teaching position at the Mechanics' Institute in New York, however, that he would begin to establish his reputation as an artist and teacher.

Cornoyer's calm, lyrical depictions of the city capture the play of light along New York's most famous boulevards and parks. His compositions, reminiscent of the contemporary Pictorialist photographs of Alfred Stieglitz and Edward Steichen, offer an optimistic view of urban life, much different from the realists' exploration of the darker industrial, urban reality. A new nationalistic pride in the modern American scene brought Impressionists like Childe Hassam, Theodore Robinson, Willard Metcalf, William Merritt Chase, and Colin Campbell Cooper to New York to document the new spirit of American life. Cornoyer, much in the vein of John Henry Twachtman, was a painter of mood. His subtle palette and brushstrokes convey an atmospheric environment that changed with the seasons. Even though Cornoyer was firmly established as a successful artist, he continued teaching throughout the Northeast, eventually retiring to East Gloucester, Massachusetts.[1]

Cornoyer's power to express the beauty of the city after a rainstorm raises the mundane to poetic grandeur. Pedestrians and hansom cabs maneuver their way through Madison Square Park along wet streets that reflect their movements. Similarly, the delicate tree branches, silhouetted against the brick and stone buildings along 23rd Street, form abstract patterns in the glistening foreground. Preferring the picturesque elements of the city, Cornoyer painted in a subdued manner that cast a veil over it and masked the chaos and discord generally associated with modern urban living.

---

1 Biographical material taken from Ira Spanierman Gallery file on the artist; *Paul Cornoyer: American Impressionist*, Exhib. cat. (Peoria: Lakeview Center for the Arts and Sciences, 1973); and Michael David Zellman, *American Art Analog*, vol. 3 (New York: Chelsea House Publishers, 1986), 599.

# *Elliot Daingerfield*

ELLIOT DAINGERFIELD, THE son of a commander in the Confederate Army, was born in Harpers Ferry, Virginia. In 1861, the family moved to Fayetteville, North Carolina, where Daingerfield apprenticed in a local china shop and photographer's studio. He left the South in 1880 for New York, where he worked first as an assistant to Walter Satterlee and then at the Art Students League. After meeting the American landscape painter George Inness in 1884, Daingerfield began to address spiritual issues in his art. From Inness, with whom he shared a studio in New York, he learned the complicated glazing techniques of the Old Masters. Albert Pinkham Ryder and Ralph Albert Blakelock also practiced Inness's technique of alternating layers of pigment and varnish to create a rich surface. While artists and critics in American academic circles were embracing the realistic naturalism that celebrated material bounty, European artists were advocating Symbolism, a rising art movement that replaced observation with an inward examination of the soul. Daingerfield was also influenced by the Barbizon school's view of nature and the application of paint. Nicknamed the "American Millet," he infused his pastoral landscapes with an arcadian stillness characteristic of Jean-François Millet, who was famous for his images of peasants and rural landscapes. Daingerfield's emotional response to painting and prose was influenced by the deaths of the two people most important to him: his wife in 1891, during childbirth, and his friend and mentor George Inness three years later. In one of the artist's many publications, he defined art as "a principle flowing out of God through certain men and women by which they perceive and understand the beautiful. The office of the artist is to express the beautiful."[1] Late in his career, he turned away from overt religious imagery and executed landscapes at his studio in Blowing Rock, North Carolina. These intimate, rich views pay homage both to the teachings of Inness and to Daingerfield's own spirituality.[2]

*Still-Life* assimilates the interest in the work of the Barbizon school artists in the ideal state of nature and traditional still-life. Daingerfield's painting presents a humble indoor celebration of the simple life. A plain silver bowl houses an abundance of garden flowers that spill into the foreground. The plentitude suggests nature's bounty, while the casual arrangement and earthen ground denote a modest interior. Although Daingerfield selected plain tableware, his painterly touch is anything but crude. He masterfully transforms an unadorned copper teapot into a rich, golden surface reminiscent of more elaborate accouterments. Similarly, the plain green cloth draped in the background is enriched by golden hues that give the composition a sense of depth.

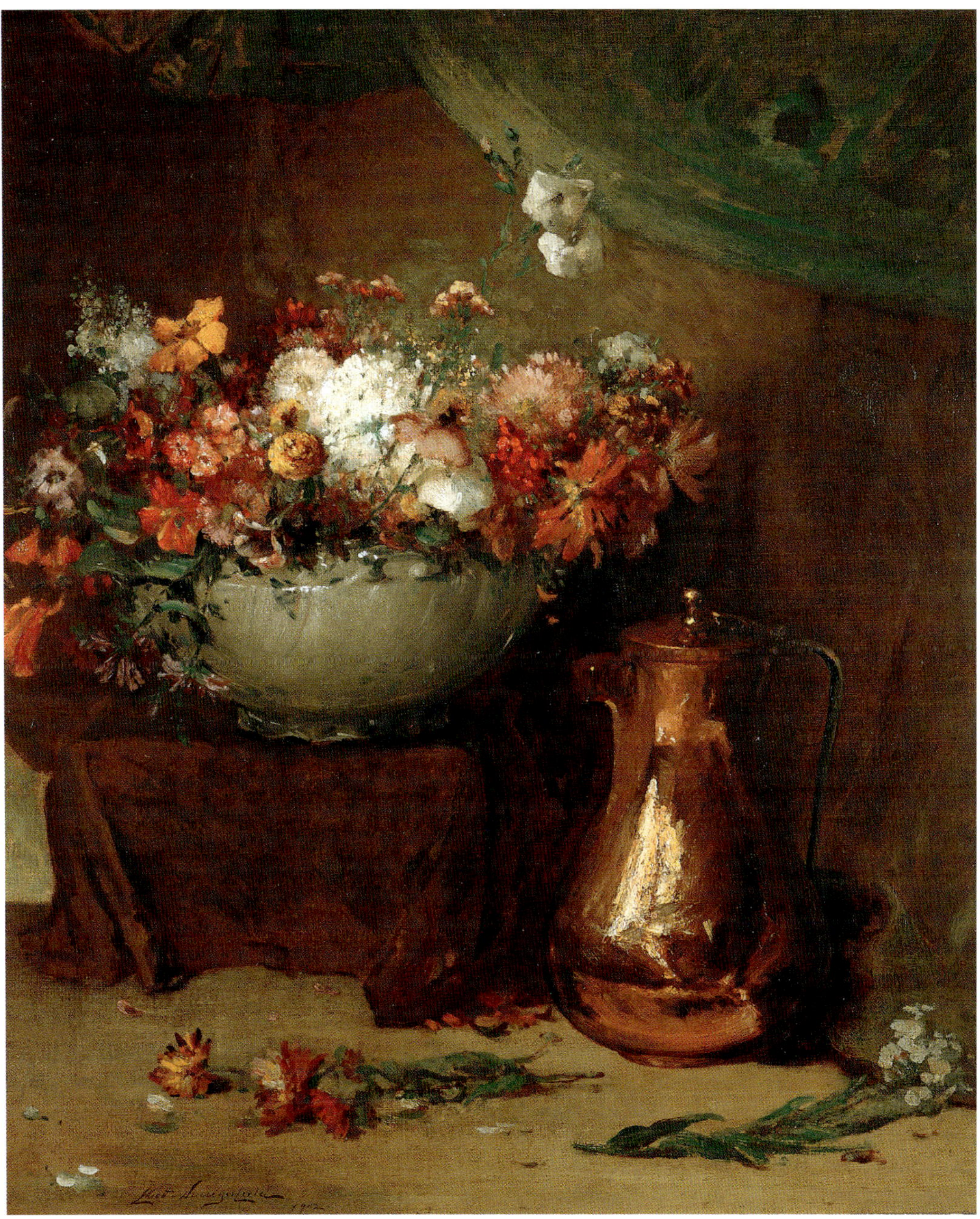

~ **No. 11** ~

ELLIOT DAINGERFIELD (AMERICAN, 1859-1932), *Still-Life*, 1902.
Oil on canvas, 28 x 24 inches. Collection of Mr. and Mrs. Dave Knoke.

---

1 Daingerfield, "Sketch of His Life–Written by Elliot Daingerfield–in Response to a Request," undated manuscript, Elliot Daingerfield Papers, Center for the Study of Southern Painting, Morris Museum of Art, quoted in Martha R. Severens, *Greenville County Museum of Art: The Southern Collection* (New York: Hudson Hills Press, 1995), 92.

2 Biographical information taken from George Inness, Jr., *Life, Art and Letters of George Inness,* with an introduction by Elliot Daingerfield (New York: The Century Company, 1917); ibid., 92; and Michael David Zellman, *American Art Analog,* vol. 2 (New York: Chelsea House Publishers, 1986), 556.

# Joseph DeCamp

AT THE AGE OF FIFTEEN, JOSEPH De Camp began his studies at Cincinnati's McMicken School of Design under the academic portrait painter Thomas S. Noble. In 1878, he traveled with William Merritt Chase and John Henry Twachtman to Munich to study under Wilhelm Diez at the Royal Academy. De Camp remained in Europe until 1882, spending his last two years studying with Frank Duveneck, whom he had met five years earlier in Cincinnati. De Camp returned to Cincinnati via Naples and London, where he visited his friend and colleague James McNeill Whistler. Upon his return, De Camp held a number of teaching positions before settling in Boston as an instructor at the School of the Museum of Fine Arts in 1895. He enjoyed enormous success with what critics called his "fancy figure portraits," often of his family and friends. In 1897, De Camp became a founding member of The Ten, a group of American Impressionist painters. His more traditional style, rooted in academia, seems disconnected from the loose brushwork and high-keyed color of his colleagues' work. While he experimented with *plein-air* landscapes during his periodic visits to Gloucester, De Camp remained heavily influenced by the realism of the Munich school. His portraiture was increasingly in demand, and his teaching position at the Normal Art School in Boston, which he held from 1903 until his death, allowed him time to advance his careeer as a portraitist, in which he achieved considerable success.[1]

*Ted* is one of the three portraits De Camp submitted to the exhibition of The Ten in 1903. Painted in his studio in Medford, Massachusetts, this portrait of his only son brilliantly captures the melancholy mood of a young boy confined indoors. Ted, shown in profile looking longingly outside, modeled for his father after a canceled trip to the Boston Navy Yard to see the arrival of the Atlantic Fleet. The subdued palette and mottled background blurred by the rain add to the rather depressed mood of the composition. Reviewers at the time noted that the three portraits exhibited a strong sense of handling and a convincing character analysis, but they also deemed the renderings "sober" and stern in feeling.[2] De Camp, like most of the painters of the Boston school, retained the tight drawing and the controlled brushwork that he had learned in Europe. He and his colleagues represent the most conservative aspect of American Impressionism.

---

1 Biographical material taken from Laurene Buckley, "Joseph De Camp," in *Ten American Painters*, Exhib. cat. (New York: Spanierman Gallery, 1990), 93-7; and Gerdts, *Masterworks of American Impressionism from the Pfeil Collection*, 106.

2 "The Ten American Painters," *Mail and Express*, 20 April 1903, 6, quoted in Buckley, 97.

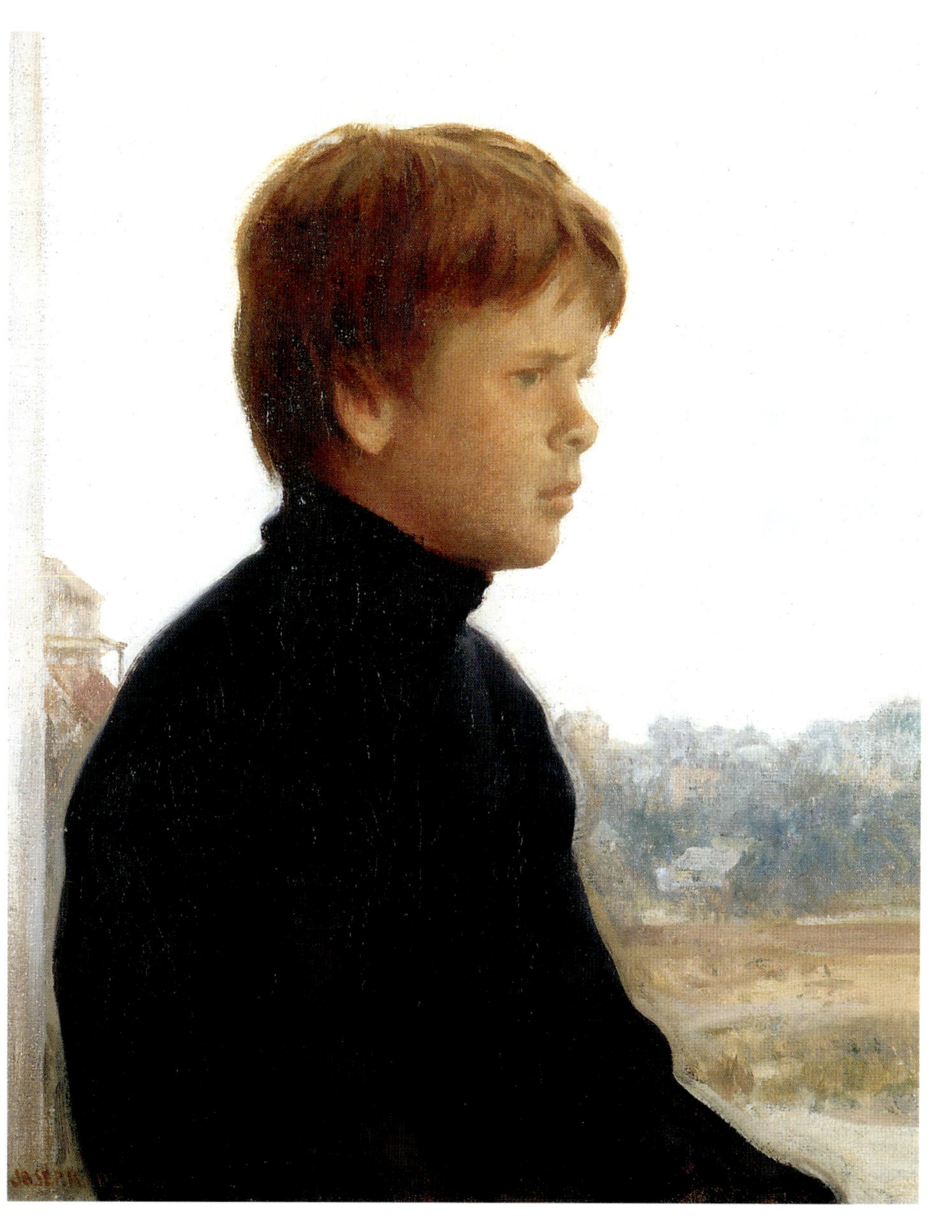

~ **No. 12** ~

Joseph De Camp (American, 1858-1923)
*Ted,* 1902
Oil on canvas
24 x 20 inches
Collection of Mr. and Mrs. Jack Huber

# Lamar Dodd

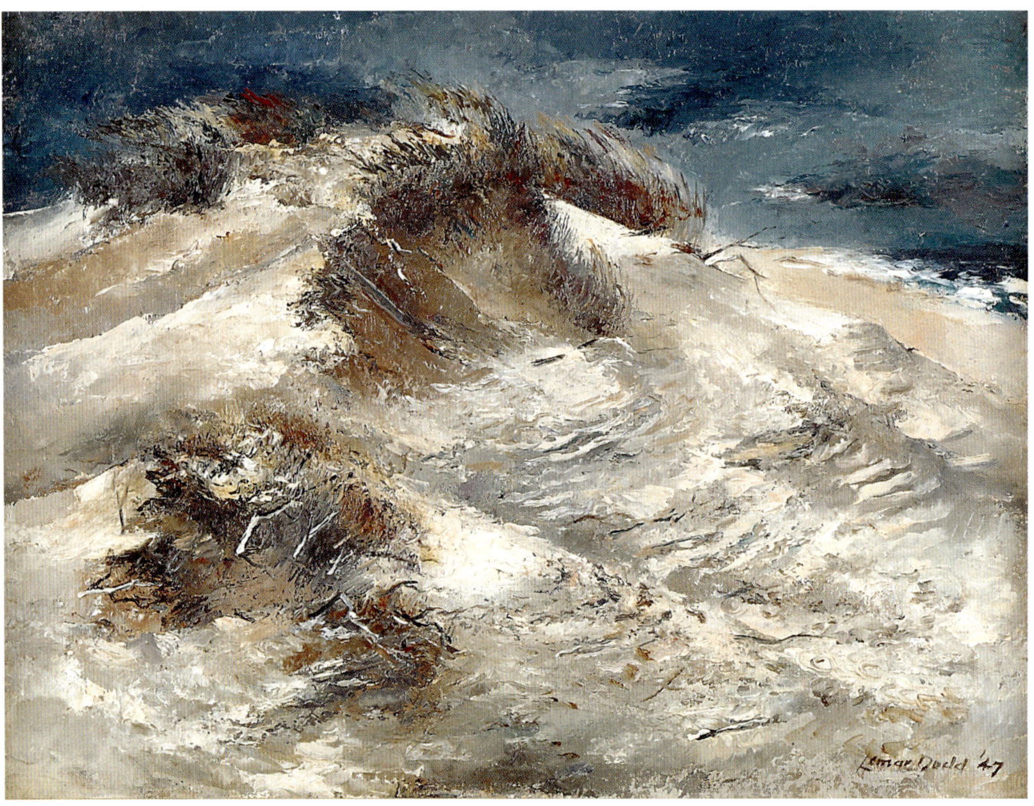


~ **No. 13** ~

LAMAR DODD (AMERICAN, 1909-1996)
*Dunes, Pawley Island*, 1947
Oil on canvas
18 x 24 inches
Collection of C.L. Morehead, Jr.

An untiring advocate and supporter of the arts in Georgia, Lamar Dodd distinguished himself as an artist, administrator, and teacher. As a youth, he exhibited an immediate fascination with his natural surroundings and an intuitive talent for art. His mother's alma mater, LaGrange Female Academy, admitted the ambitious twelve-year-old to the all-female school in exchange for lawn service and provided him with his first instruction in art. Dodd quickly advanced beyond the teaching capabilities of the academy and, in 1926, left in search of collegiate experience. He enrolled in the School of Architecture at the Georgia Institute of Technology but was bored with the tedious requirements of the program. In 1928, he abandoned architecture for painting and moved to New York and enrolled at the Art Students League, where he met and studied with some of the leading forces in American art.

In 1937, Dodd left New York to accept a position as the head of the University of Georgia's art department. Although much of his tenure was spent building the reputation of the art department, Dodd continued to develop his artistic style. He traveled extensively throughout the United States as a visiting artist and guest lecturer in the 1940s, and to Europe and the Near East as a representative of various governmental agencies in the 1950s. Dodd's palette and brushstroke became looser and more expressive, yet he never abandoned the representational in his art. From the regional scenes he painted in New York to the abstracted series of paintings executed abroad, Dodd always sought to reveal the spiritual essence of his subject.[1] His foray into the universal continued over the next two decades with the creation of two definitive series. In 1963, Dodd was invited to witness the inner workings of the space program as an official artist of NASA. Art historian Lloyd Goodrich succinctly labeled the resulting space series as "the freest and boldest of [Dodd's] entire career." Ten years later, Dodd journeyed from deep space to the human body in his series *The Heart.* His aesthetic investigation stands as a memorial to his wife, who died in 1986 after open-heart surgery. From the macrocosm to the microcosm, the regional to the universal, Dodd's career spanned the realism of the period before World War II to the abstraction of the years surrounding America's technological advances into space as well as medicine.[2]

In his seascapes, Dodd, nicknamed "a master of mood," conveyed a sense of raw energy and palpable atmosphere. Executed in 1947, *Dunes, Pawley Island* communicates Dodd's direct experience of the shore of South Carolina. A reduced palette, vigorous brushstroke, and the artist's selective eye focus on the elemental power of nature. The landscapes that Dodd painted during the years immediately following World War II show a native in touch with his roots. In these pictures, whether of the mountains or the seashore, Dodd expressed a love for the beauty of a region that had been so impoverished by the Depression only a decade earlier.

1 William U. Eiland, *The Truth in Things* (Athens: The University of Georgia Press, 1996).

2 Biographical information taken from Emily Ann Arthur, ed., *Lamar Dodd: The C.L. Morehead, Jr. Collection* (Athens: Privately published, 1996); and Eiland.

# Frank Duveneck

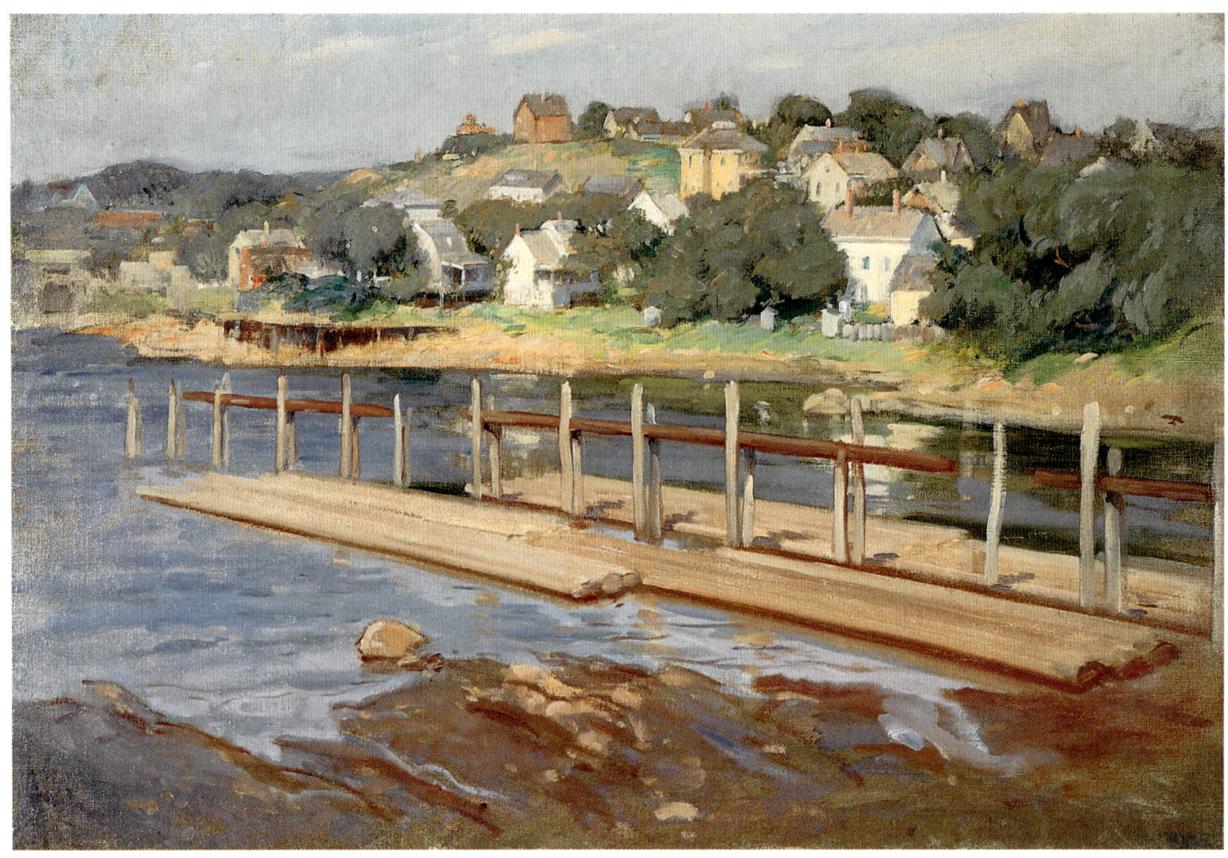

~ **No. 14** ~

FRANK DUVENECK (AMERICAN, 1848-1919)
*Small Boat Landing*, ca. 1913
Oil on canvas
24 x 36 inches
Collection of Mrs. Edward L. McConnell

BORN FRANCIS DECKER IN Covington, Kentucky, in 1848, Frank Duveneck later adopted the surname of his stepfather, Joseph Duveneck. Both his mother and stepfather had recently relocated from northern Germany and raised Frank within Cincinnati's large community of German immigrants. Due to the language and cultural barriers between the German-speaking Duveneck and the mainstream art community, the young artist began his career as a church decorator with the newly established Institute of Catholic Art.[1] Originally intending to continue church decoration in Munich, Duveneck changed his plans after arriving in Germany and enrolled in painting classes at the prestigious Bavarian Royal Academy in 1870. He worked under Wilhelm Diez, who introduced the artist to the work of the renowned realist painter Wilhelm Liebl. Duveneck quickly adopted the dark tonalities and vigorous brushwork characteristic of the Munich realists. John Singer Sargent, a fellow student at the academy, described Duveneck as "the greatest talent of the brush of this generation."[2] By the late 1870s, Duveneck had formed his own school for American art students. His followers, referred to affectionately as the "Duveneck boys," included John Henry Twachtman, Joseph De Camp, and William Merritt Chase. The school moved from Munich to Italy in 1879, and Duveneck's subject matter shifted from portraiture to *plein-air* landscapes. His characteristic dark palette brightened and his brushstroke softened as he painted the picturesque harbors and architecture of Venice. Duveneck, who remained in Europe for more than half of his career, returned to Cincinnati only for brief stays. When he arrived in 1889, he did so with an established reputation as an effective teacher and talented artist. Duveneck taught at the Cincinnati Art Museum and the Art Academy of Cincinnati. During his later years, he spent his summers in Gloucester, Massachusetts, where he created numerous *plein-air* seascapes.[3]

*Small Boat Landing* is a view of Banner Hill in Gloucester. Duveneck maintained a studio on either side of the harbor that granted him different vantage points from which to paint. One allowed him to capture the morning sun; the other he used for views of the afternoon and evening light. His use of brighter local colors and an impressionistic style can be attributed in part to his association with fellow Gloucester painters Willard Metcalf and Childe Hassam, members of The Ten. The white and yellow cottages that line the shore seem to soak up the sun and cast their bright reflections upon the water. Even the decaying dock, which juts diagonally into the harbor, appears bleached by the brilliant sunshine.

1 Michael Quick, *An American Painter Abroad: Frank Duveneck's European Years*, Exhib. cat. (Cincinnati: Cincinnati Art Museum, 1987), 11.

2 Gwendolyn Owens and John Peters-Campbell, *Golden Day–Silver Night: Perceptions of Nature in American Art, 1850-1910* (Ithaca: Cornell University Press, 1982), 44.

3 Biographical material taken from Robert Neuhaus, *Unsuspected Genius: The Art and Life of Frank Duveneck* (San Francisco: Bedford Press, 1987); and Quick.

# Ellen Thayer Fisher & Abbott H. Thayer

Ellen (Nelly) Thayer Fisher and her brother, the prominent American artist Abbott H. Thayer, were raised in Keene, New Hampshire. The Thayer children were avid nature lovers whose early interest in botany and taxidermy anticipated the dominant themes of their later work. Fisher's father, a physician, relocated the family to Brooklyn, New York, in 1867, after his service in the Civil War. While her brother attended the Brooklyn Art School and later the National Academy of Design, Fisher benefited only from Abbott's advice and criticism. Nineteenth-century women were encouraged to practice art as a genteel pastime. Flora and fauna were deemed suitable subject matter for women, and watercolor was recommended for its gentler appearance and ease of execution. While Fisher painted within the narrow constructs of propriety, she differentiated herself from other female artists by her critical and commercial success. Fisher exhibited at the Brooklyn Art Association regularly from 1867 to 1884 and signed a contract with the Prang Company of Boston, which transformed her designs into greeting cards. Her work was exhibited in Philadelphia at the United States International Exposition in 1876 and in five annual exhibitions of the National Academy of Design between 1868 and 1880. Her father noted in the Thayer family journal that Fisher "reproduced most faithfully the character of her models and evinced a delicate color sense, and power of composition."[1]

*Nesting Bird in Apple Blossoms* is a collaborative effort by Fisher and her brother. Fisher is responsible for the watercolor depiction of the apple blossoms executed on paper; Thayer painted in oil a nest with birds and signed "A.H. Thayer" on an adjacent branch. The work was most likely painted between 1900 and 1909, when Thayer was interested in themes of natural camouflage. During these years, while working collaboratively with his children and other artists, he created compositions in which animals blend into their natural habitats. Fisher's apple blossoms resemble the work of several other female artists in New York and Boston, including noted still-life painter Ellen Robbins.

---

1 Biographical information taken from Ross Anderson, *Abbott Handerson Thayer* (New York: Everson Museum, 1982).

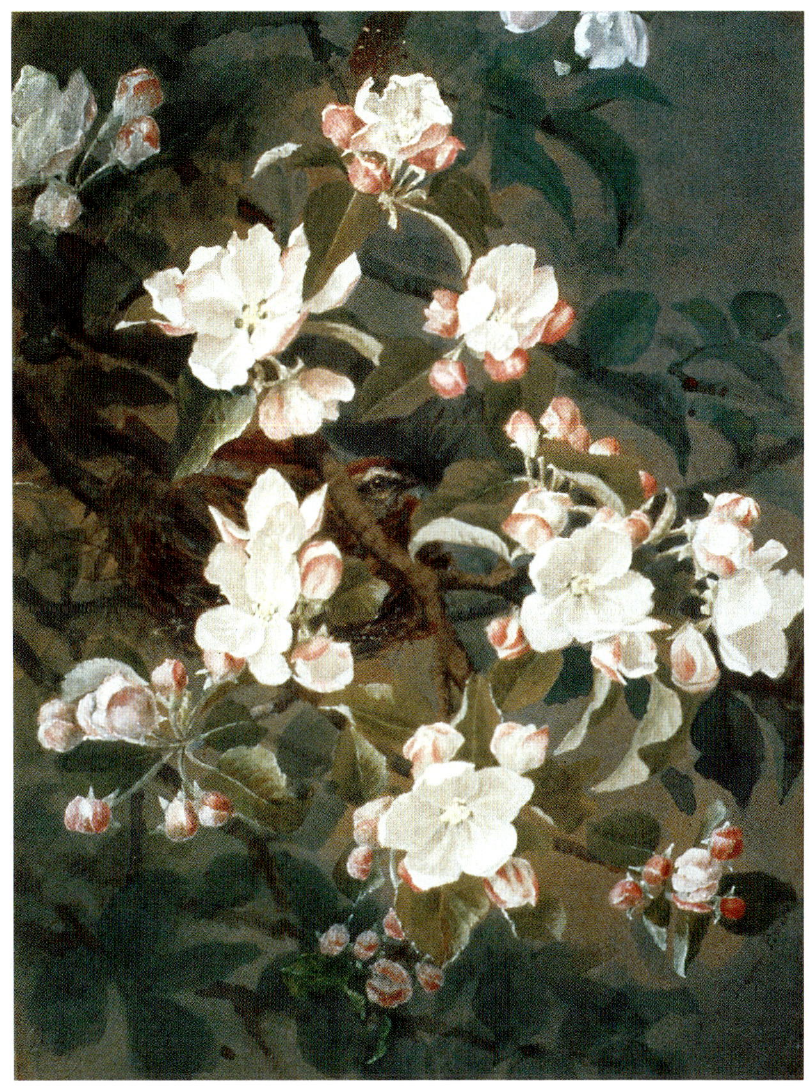

**No. 15**

ELLEN THAYER FISHER (AMERICAN, 1847-1911)
AND ABBOTT H. THAYER (AMERICAN, 1849-1921)
*Nesting Bird in Apple Blossoms*
Watercolor and oil on paper
12 x 9 inches
The Sellars Collection

# Sanford Gifford

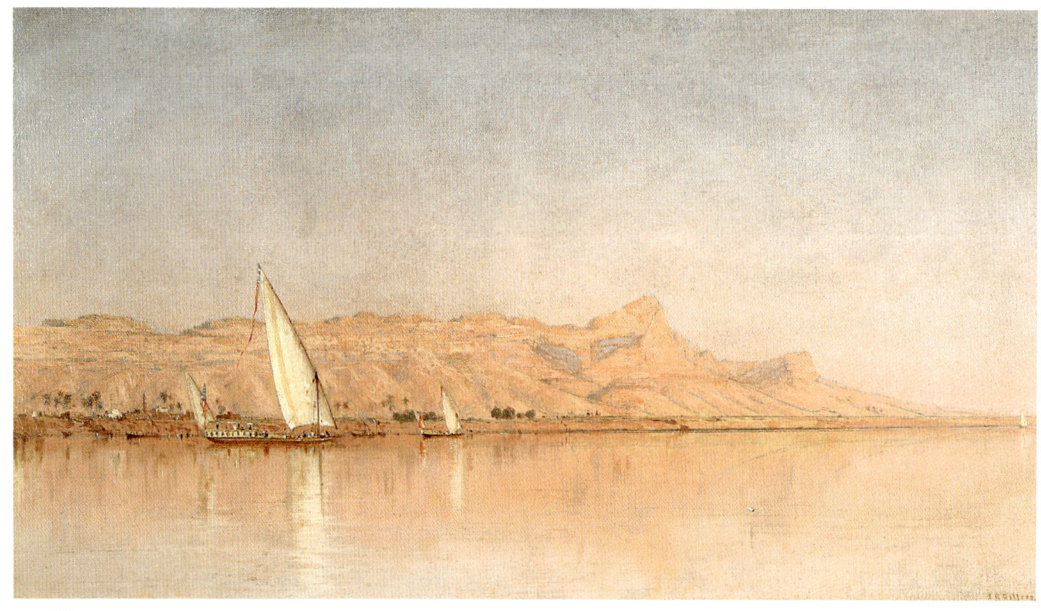

No. 16

SANFORD GIFFORD (AMERICAN, 1823-1880), *On the Nile*, 1872.
Oil on canvas, 16 ½ x 30 ¾ inches. Collection of Mr. and Mrs. Holcombe Green.

SANFORD ROBINSON GIFFORD was born into a wealthy New York family and lived near the scenic Catskill Mountains and Hudson River. He attended Brown University but left in 1844 to study art. Gifford initially studied portraiture under the accomplished though largely unknown draftsman John Smith but quickly turned to landscape, which later dominated his oeuvre. He stated, "Having once enjoyed the absolute freedom of the Landscape Painter's life I was unable to return to portrait painting." [1] In 1851, Gifford was named an associate of the National Academy of Design and three years later became an academician. Gifford spent two years touring Europe. His journey, much in the spirit of the acclaimed Grand Tour of the eighteenth century, was intended to acquaint Gifford with the European masters and spiritual aspects of European scenery. He often traveled with Albert Bierstadt and Worthington Whittredge on walking tours and captured in paint some of the most remote, picturesque settings of Europe. Gifford returned to America and opened a studio on Tenth Street in New York. After serving with the Seventh New York Regiment during the Civil War, Gifford returned to Europe in 1868-69 and spent another year exploring the Continent and the Middle East. His poetic sensibility found a natural home with the exotic culture and shimmering light found in the Eastern landscapes. He and painter Martin Johnson Heade were instrumental in establishing the now-called Luminist style, which presented a contemplative view of nature. Their otherworldly depictions conveyed an interest in Transcendentalism through a harmonious blending of light, removal of visible brushstroke, strong horizontal compositions, and small canvases.[2]

Gifford took a six-week, thousand-mile excursion up the Nile in January 1869. The travel writer George William Curtis wrote poetically of his similar tour taken a few years earlier: "For the dream-days dawn-lotus-eating days of faith in the poets as the only practical people , because all the world is poetry . . . days that dissolve the world in light. The azure air and azure water mingle." [3] *On the Nile* is a superb example of the mature Luminist aesthetic, whose antecedents can be found in the Romantic landscapes of the German painter Caspar David Friedrich. Shortly before the style gained favor in America, it found adherents in northern Europe and Great Britain, notably in the paintings of Danes Christian Ekersberg and Christian Købke, German Maximillian Hausofer, and British painters John Bret and Edward Lear. The Americans combined a Nordic spiritualism and mystical light and the popular attention to detail found in paintings of the Pre-Raphaelite Brotherhood.[4]

Gifford's painting of the Nile garnered praise from critics at the Brooklyn Art Association exhibition in December 1872:

> *Mr. S. R. Gifford . . . shows by his "On the Nile" how his love for certain effects of light can develop new force in him when it has undeniable conditions of nature to work upon. His former pictures were never completely satisfactory because we could not find their justification in American scenery from which they professed to be taken. But here on the Nile the artist has found an atmosphere that suits his talent, and we wish we may see an abundant record of his observations.* [5]

---

1 Sanford Gifford to Rev. O.B. Frothingham, quoted in Ila Weiss, *Poetic Landscape: The Art and Experience of Sanford R. Gifford* (Newark: University of Delaware Press, 1987), 46.

2 Biographical material taken from ibid.; Ila Weiss, "Sanford R. Gifford in Europe: A Sketchbook of 1868," *American Art Journal* 9 (1977): 83-103; and John Wilmerding, *American Light: The Luminist Movement, 1850-1875*, Exhib. cat. (Washington, D.C.: National Gallery of Art, 1980).

3 George William Curtis, *Nile Notes of a Howadji* (New York: Harper and Brothers, 1854): 6, quoted in Weiss, 121.

4 See Theodore E. Stebbins, Jr., "Luminism in Context: A New View," *American Light*: 211-36.

5 Weiss, 136.

# *Richard LaBarre Goodwin*

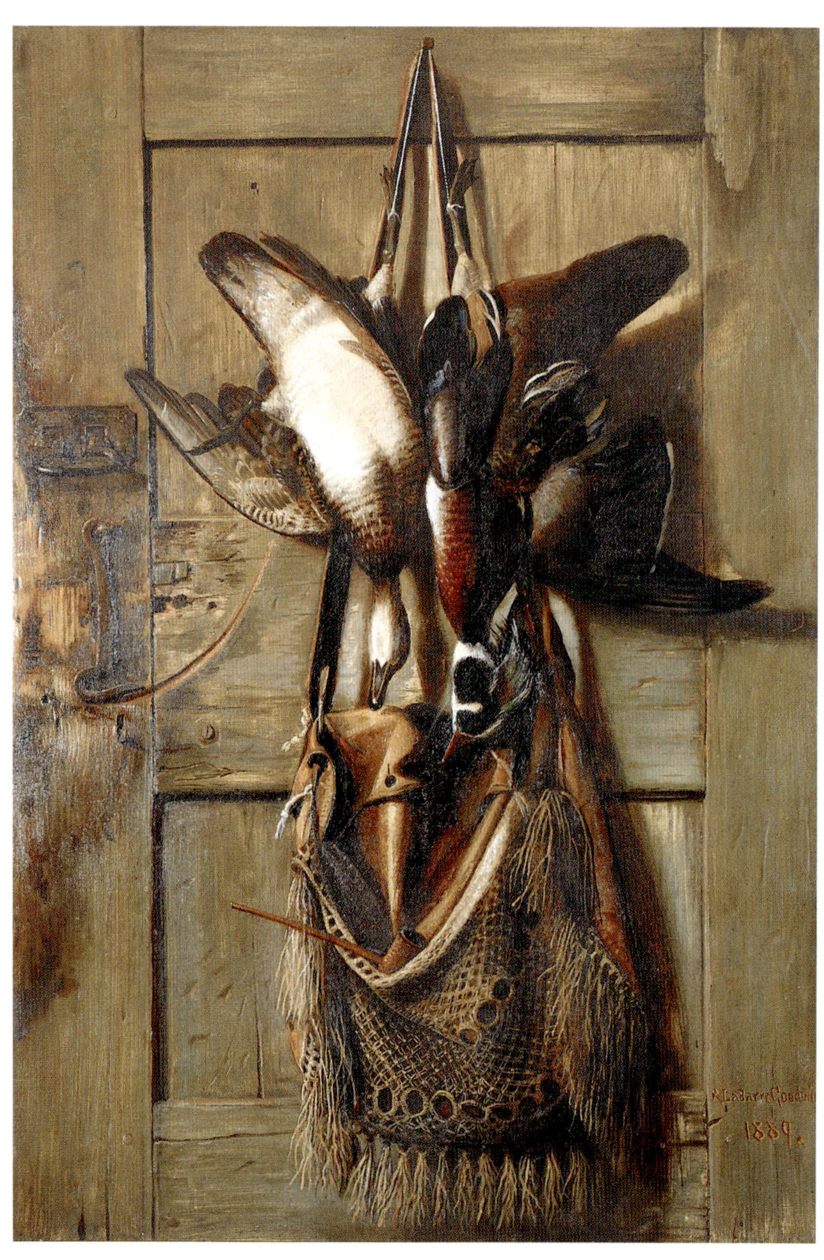

~ **No. 17** ~

RICHARD LABARRE GOODWIN
(AMERICAN, 1840-1910)
*After the Hunt*, 1889
Oil on board
40 x 28 inches
Collection of Mr. and Mrs.
Fred D. Bentley, Sr.

RICHARD LABARRE GOODWIN, the son of prolific portrait painter Edwin Weyburn Goodwin, was born in Albany, New York. Studying with relatively unknown artists during his youth, Goodwin chose the commercially successful field of portraiture. He traveled throughout New York and spent time in Ithaca, Seneca Falls, Clifton Springs, and Rochester. In the 1880s, he set up a studio in Syracuse, where he executed his first still-lifes. Goodwin never settled too long in one place, however, and by 1890, he had moved to Washington, D.C., where his patrons included senators and foreign dignitaries. Later, he explored the rugged terrain of Colorado, California, and Oregon, where he hunted, fished, and took long pack trips into the wilderness. Goodwin spent his final years in New York.[1]

While he continued to paint portraits throughout his career, Goodwin is remembered today as a painter of hanging game and cabin-door still-lifes. He first experimented with cabin-door still-lifes after witnessing William Harnett's successful debut of a trompe-l'oeil cabin door in New York's Stewart Salon in 1886. Although both artists adopted the theme of the hunting door, the differences in their backgrounds are reflected in the types of items they chose to include. Harnett, an urban dweller, generally included rare, expensive, collector-quality guns and knives that hung illusionistically from richly painted doors, while Goodwin appealed to the true hunter by depicting unpretentious items intended for use instead of display.

*After the Hunt* is an excellent example of Goodwin's talent for deceiving the eye. The battered, unpainted cabin door and rusted hinge and hook became staples of Goodwin's compositions. While he varied the objects, Goodwin favored the central columnar organization, which allowed him to show more of the door and contain his subject matter within a simplified arrangement. In the present example, Goodwin chose a string of ducks that arch above the intricately painted game bag. The delicate white breast of the female contrasts with the vibrantly colored feathers of her mate. A simple cork pipe, balancing precariously within the worn leather crease of the bag and inviting the viewer to pick it up, completes Goodwin's illusion. One similarly feels compelled to trace Goodwin's carved signature and date in the lower right corner of the door. During the late nineteenth century, the concept of reality was being challenged from all directions as the perceptions of time and space were being fundamentally altered. Goodwin successfully tricks the viewer into thinking this painting is indeed a "real" door.

---

1 Biographical material taken from Alfred Frankenstein, *After the Hunt: William Harnett and Other American Still Life Painters, 1870-1900* (Berkeley: University of California Press, 1969); Alfred Frankenstein, *The Reality of Appearance: The Trompe-L'Oeil Tradition in American Painting* (New York: New York Graphic Society, Ltd., 1970); William H. Gerdts and Russell Burke, *American Still-Life Painting* (New York: Praeger Publishers, 1971).

# *Philip Leslie Hale*

Philip Leslie Hale was born into a prominent Boston family and was intended from an early age to attend Harvard University. Much to his father's dismay, however, Hale rejected university life for art school and eventually became one of the most interesting yet under-recognized figure painters in Boston. With the support of his aunt, the artist Susan Hale, Philip entered the School of the Museum of Fine Arts in 1883. He then studied at the Art Students League in New York and in 1887 traveled to Paris to attend the Académie Julian and the Ecole des Beaux-Arts. Under the direction of Gustave Boulanger, Jules-Joseph Lefebvre, and Henri-Lucien Doucet, Hale acquired a firm grasp of the academic principles of figure painting. During the 1890s, he joined other American expatriates in Giverny and adopted the Impressionist aesthetic. Upon his return to America, he taught life drawing at his alma mater, the School of the Museum of Fine Arts, and art history at Boston University. In 1913, he began teaching studio classes at the Pennsylvania Academy of the Fine Arts. "Très Impressioniste" is how Hale described his style in a letter to colleague William Howard Hart; however, his luminous visions of white-clad young ladies painted in garden settings were far more translucent than those of his fellow Impressionist artists.[1]

Critics were unsure of the artist's unusual palette and diaphanous forms and offered mixed reviews of his exhibition at the Durand-Ruel Gallery in New York in 1895. By the turn of the century, Hale returned to his original training and began creating compositions more firmly rooted in the academic aesthetic. His marriage in 1902 to Lilian Westcott Hale, herself an able figure painter, may also have influenced the artist's mature style.[2]

*Girl with a Golden Cane* was most likely completed after 1900, when Hale was becoming more conservative in his style. Here, Hale places his young model solidly in her wooden chair, cloaked in all the finery appropriate to the Boston elite. Some links with Impressionism, however, can still be discerned in the vigorous brushwork and coloristic details of the young girl's attire. Despite her conservative pose, the young woman gazes boldly at the viewer. Her delicately upturned hand and seductive gaze hold the viewer in a manner quite unusual for tradition-bound painters in Boston at the time.

---

1 Letter to William Howard Hart, 1895, quoted in Gerdts, *American Impressionism*, 119.

2 Biographical information taken from Trevor J. Fairbrother, *The Bostonians: Painters of an Elegant Age, 1870-1930* (Boston: Northeastern University Press, 1986).

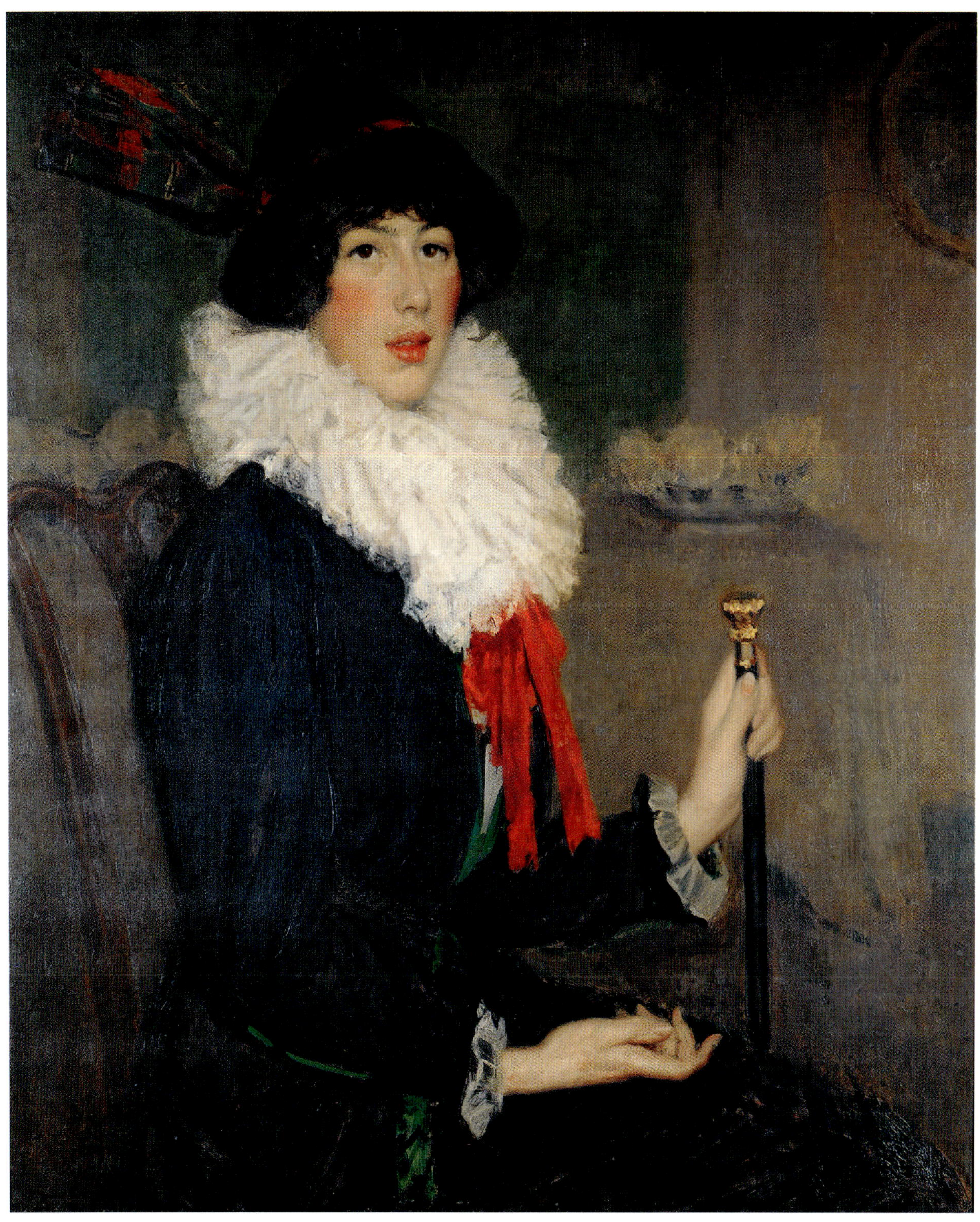

~ **No. 18** ~

Philip Leslie Hale (American, 1865-1931), *Girl with a Golden Cane*.
Oil on canvas, 36 x 30 inches. Collection of Mr. and Mrs. Noel Wadsworth.

# *Hamilton Hamilton*

HAMILTON HAMILTON gained his initial training in landscape painting at the American artists' colony in Pont-Aven, France, in 1870. The school's aesthetic philosophy joined the Romantic influences of the French Barbizon school with the pastoral naturalism of English painter John Constable. Hamilton's resulting landscapes demonstrated a subjective understanding of nature that relied more on mood than topographical accuracy. Soon after his arrival in Europe, he was called back to his adopted home of Buffalo, New York, to help support his family; thus began his lucrative business as a portrait painter. Little is known of this period except that Hamilton was elected an associate member of the National Academy of Design and became a full member in 1889. Twenty-five years after his initial training in France, Hamilton returned to Europe, this time working along the coast of Great Britian. During his two-year sojourn in England, Hamilton formed an important association with the renowned English critic and aesthete Sir John Ruskin, who played a dominant role in the creation of American taste during the mid-nineteenth century and championed the art of the Pre-Raphaelite painters, whose highly detailed paintings reflect their reverence for nature, the early Renaissance, and Platonic beauty. By the turn of the century, Hamilton had embraced Ruskin's ideas and ideals. He returned to New York in 1896, but because of ailing health sought respite on the West Coast. The comfort Hamilton found in the California sun was reflected in his paintings, which were increasingly characterized by a lighter palette and a freer use of color.

*Woman with Fan* demonstrates Hamilton's exposure to the ideas and aesthetics of Ruskin. The composition exemplifies British Victorian painting and extols its ideal of pure beauty. Hamilton depicted a fair young woman standing alone with her demure face slightly hidden by a fan. She dominates the composition, yet her complementary coloring blends into the vaguely defined earthy environment, forming the age-old association of woman and nature. Hamilton, like his Pre-Raphaelite predecessors, avoided depicting the modern industrialized world and instead returns the viewer to an arcadian past, yet one full of the ornamentation so favored by Victorians. Hamilton's subject appears content to remain in a world untouched by modern reality.

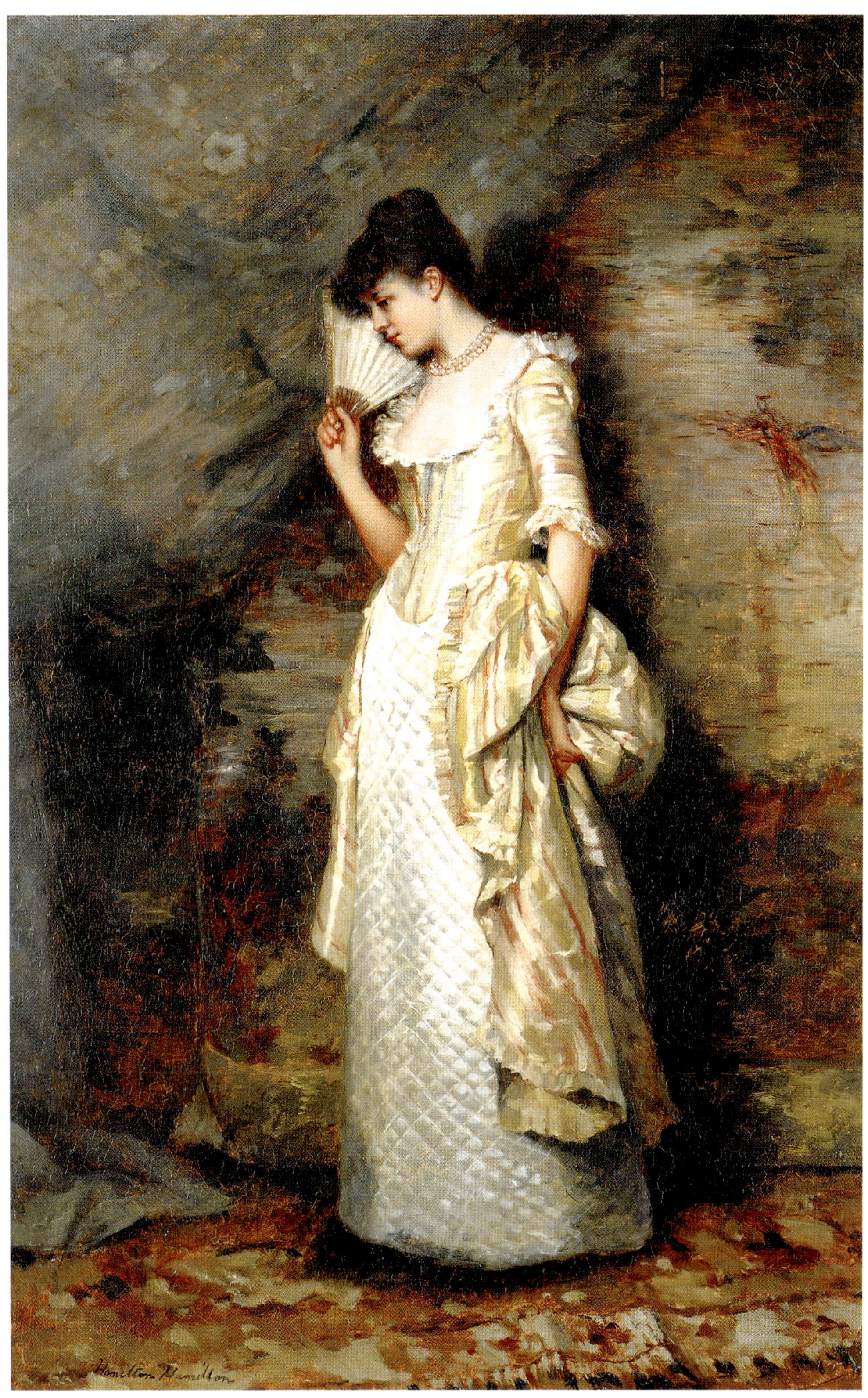


**No. 19**

HAMILTON HAMILTON
(ENGLISH, 1847-1928)
*Woman with Fan*, ca. 1900
Oil on Masonite
30 x 19 ⅞ inches
Collection of Mr. and Mrs.
R. Randall Bentley, Sr.

# Charles W. Hawthorne

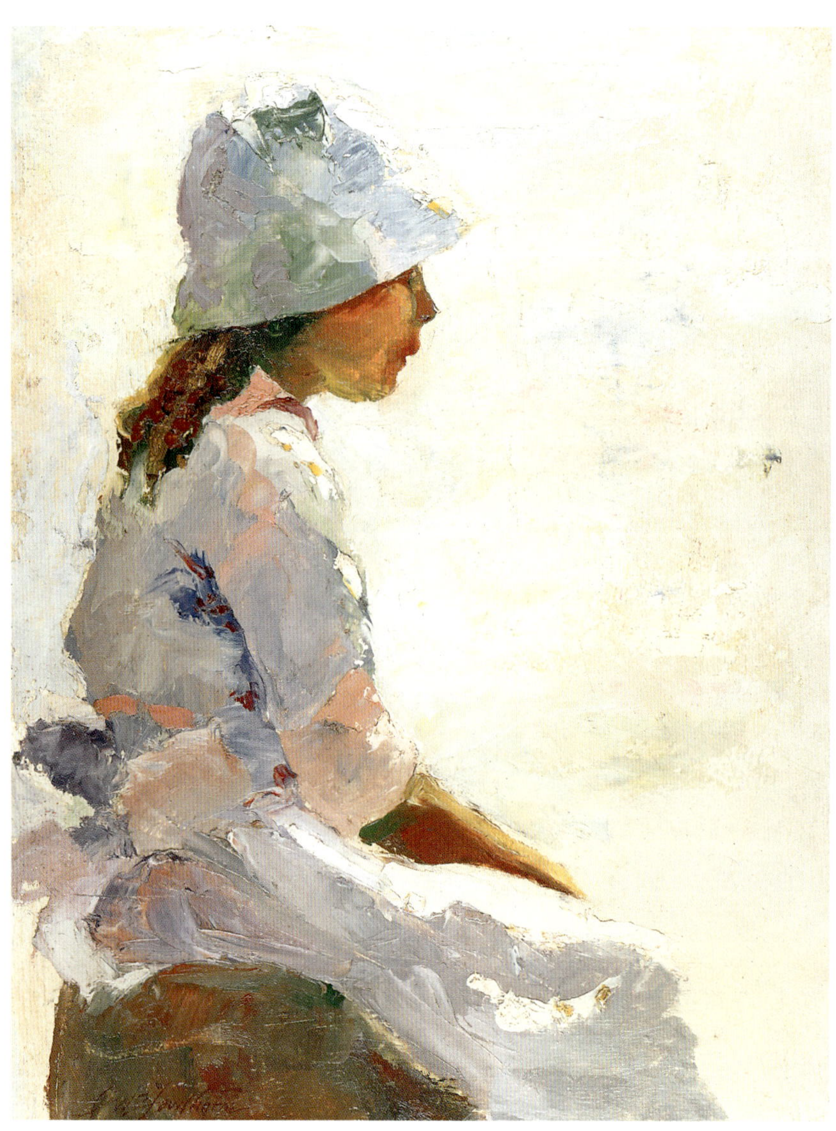

~ **No. 20** ~

CHARLES W. HAWTHORNE
(AMERICAN, 1872-1930)
*At the Seaside*, ca. 1920
Oil on canvas
20 x 16 inches
Collection of Heather C. Huber

Charles Hawthorne's father, the captain of a ship employed in the coastal trade of New England, raised his son in a small town on the Kennebec River in Maine. At eighteen, Hawthorne moved to New York and enrolled at the Art Students League while supporting himself as a dock hand and later an employee at a stained-glass factory. Over the next three years, Hawthorne worked under Frank Vincent Du Mond, George de Forest Brush, and Siddons Mowbray, but it was his rather turbulent relationship with William Merritt Chase that introduced him to the Impressionist aesthetic. He studied in Chase's school at Shinnecock, Long Island, and helped organize his New York school in the fall of 1896. Two years later, Hawthorne went abroad and studied in Holland, where he painted the local villagers and fishermen, subjects which appear throughout his oeuvre. Upon his return to America, he opened his own summer school, the Cape Cod School of Art, in Provincetown, Massachusetts. Hawthorne continued to portray provincial subjects from the seaside fishing community and created striking compositions of the local fishermen. His philosophy was simple, "One of the greatest things in the world is to train ourselves to see beauty in the commonplace . . . . Anything under the sun is beautiful if you have the vision–it is the seeing of the thing that makes it so." [1] The *New York Times* praised his work: ". . . sturdy, simple and real, these figures are not merely naturalistic; they are raised above that level." In 1906, Hawthorne returned to Europe, where he spent a year in Italy. When he returned to America and settled in Provincetown, his style became increasingly abstract. He executed a series of watercolor landscapes that express the raw emotion he felt for his environs. Freely painted with broad washes of atmospheric colors, these pictures demonstrate the depth of Hawthorne's ability. [2]

Hawthorne stated to his students that "Beauty in art is the delicious notes of color one against the other," [3] thus revealing his reliance on the aesthetics of realism and Impressionism. In *At the Seaside*, Hawthorne applied broad, flattened areas of color with a palette knife to convey an abstract sense of immediacy within the composition. The brilliant sunlight is described in varying patches of white that dominate the background and highlight the young girl's hat and dress. While the subject matter is carefree, Hawthorne depicted the young girl alone, lost in a moment of thought and unaware of her audience. The psychological distance apparent in *At the Seaside* characterizes much of Hawthorne's portraiture. The press disparagingly nicknamed such detachment the "Hawthorne stare."[4]

---

1 Charles Hawthorne quoted in Marvin S. Sadek, *The Paintings of Charles Hawthorne* (University of Connecticut Museum of Art, 1968), n.p.

2 Biographical material taken from Evan Firestone, "Color and Light: The Late Watercolors of Charles W. Hawthorne," *Arts Magazine* 57 (May 1983): 136-9; and ibid.

3 Charles W. Hawthorne, *Hawthorne on Painting* (New York, 1960), quoted in Firestone, 136.

4 Sadek, n.p.

# *Robert Henri*

ROBERT HENRI, BORN ROBERT Henry Cozad in Cincinnati, Ohio, spent his early years working on his father's farm in Nebraska. After a fight erupted between a local rancher and Henri's father, the family fled to Denver in 1882 and assumed new identities. John Cozad changed his name to Robert Henry Lee; his son took the name Robert Earle Henri and was introduced as his adopted son. The family spent years dodging a murder indictment, which was later pardoned.

The raw, unspoiled environment of the West left an indelible impression on Henri, even though the family eventually settled in Atlantic City, New Jersey, in 1884. Two years later, Henri enrolled at the Pennsylvania Academy of the Fine Arts and studied under Thomas Anshutz, whose unidealized studies of the mundane activities of the laboring classes greatly influenced Henri's choice of subject matter. After two years of study, Henri left for Paris, where he enrolled at the Académie Julian from 1888 to 1891 and then briefly at the Ecole des Beaux-Arts. Henri experimented with the new Impressionist style during his first stay in Europe but on his second trip in 1895, adopted a darker realism based on the paintings of Velázquez, Hals, and Rembrandt. In 1900, Henri opened a studio in New York and actively cultivated an avant-garde circle of artists, critics, and writers, all of whom were rebelling against conventional academic thought and practice. Henri encouraged an unidealized approach to art among his students at the New York School of Art, where he taught from 1902 to 1909. He urged fellow Philadelphia artists William Glackens, George Luks, Everett Shinn, and John Sloan to join him in New York. Henri's final rejection of the repressive Academy occurred in 1908. Along with his four colleagues from Philadelphia, plus Arthur B. Davies, Ernest Lawson, and Maurice Prendergast, Henri organized an unjuried exhibition, *The Eight*, at the MacBeth Gallery in New York. This unorthodox presentation rivaled the annual juried showcase of the National Academy of Design and brought so much commercial and critical success to the members of the group that it prompted Henri to launch an even larger exhibition of the Independent Artists in 1910. The Armory Show of 1913 showcased European progressives who, like Henri, demanded innovation and experimentation of their participants. While Henri championed their cause, he never abandoned the humanistic content he believed vital to art's purpose. Henri spent his later years dividing his time between New Mexico, Ireland, and New York.[1]

Henri painted *Tewa* on one of his many trips to Santa Fe; this work represents the artist's mature style, in which he embraced Hardesty

Maratta's theories of color and design, evident in the bright palette of *Tewa*. Each brilliantly loaded brushstroke is evident on the canvas, but Henri never allowed his figure to become lost in abstraction. The young girl's humanity, vibrant beneath the radiant orange cloak, expresses her strength of character. Unlike many nineteenth- and twentieth-century artists, Henri viewed Native Americans without nostalgia and focused each image on the individual characteristics of the sitter. As he stated to his class at the Art Students League,

> ***[I] was not interested in these people to sentimentalize over them, to mourn over the fact that we have destroyed the Indian . . . . I am looking at each individual with the eager hope of finding there something of the dignity of life . . . something of the order that will rescue the race and the nation.***[2]

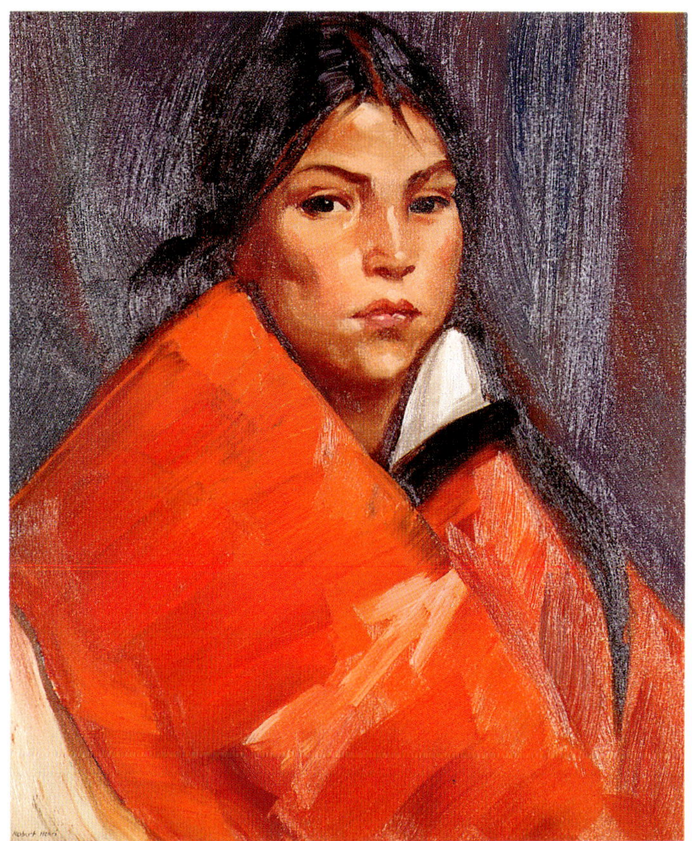

**No. 21**

ROBERT HENRI (AMERICAN, 1865-1929)
*Tewa*, 1916
Oil on canvas
24 x 20 inches
Collection of Terry and Margaret Stent

---

1 Biographical information taken from William Innes Homer, *Robert Henri and His Circle* (Ithaca: Cornell University Press, 1969); and Bennard B. Perlman, ed., *Revolutionaries of Realism: The Letters of John Sloan and Robert Henri* (Princeton: Princeton University Press, 1997).

2 Robert Henri, *The Art Spirit* (Philadelphia, 1923), 148, cited in Perlman, 244.

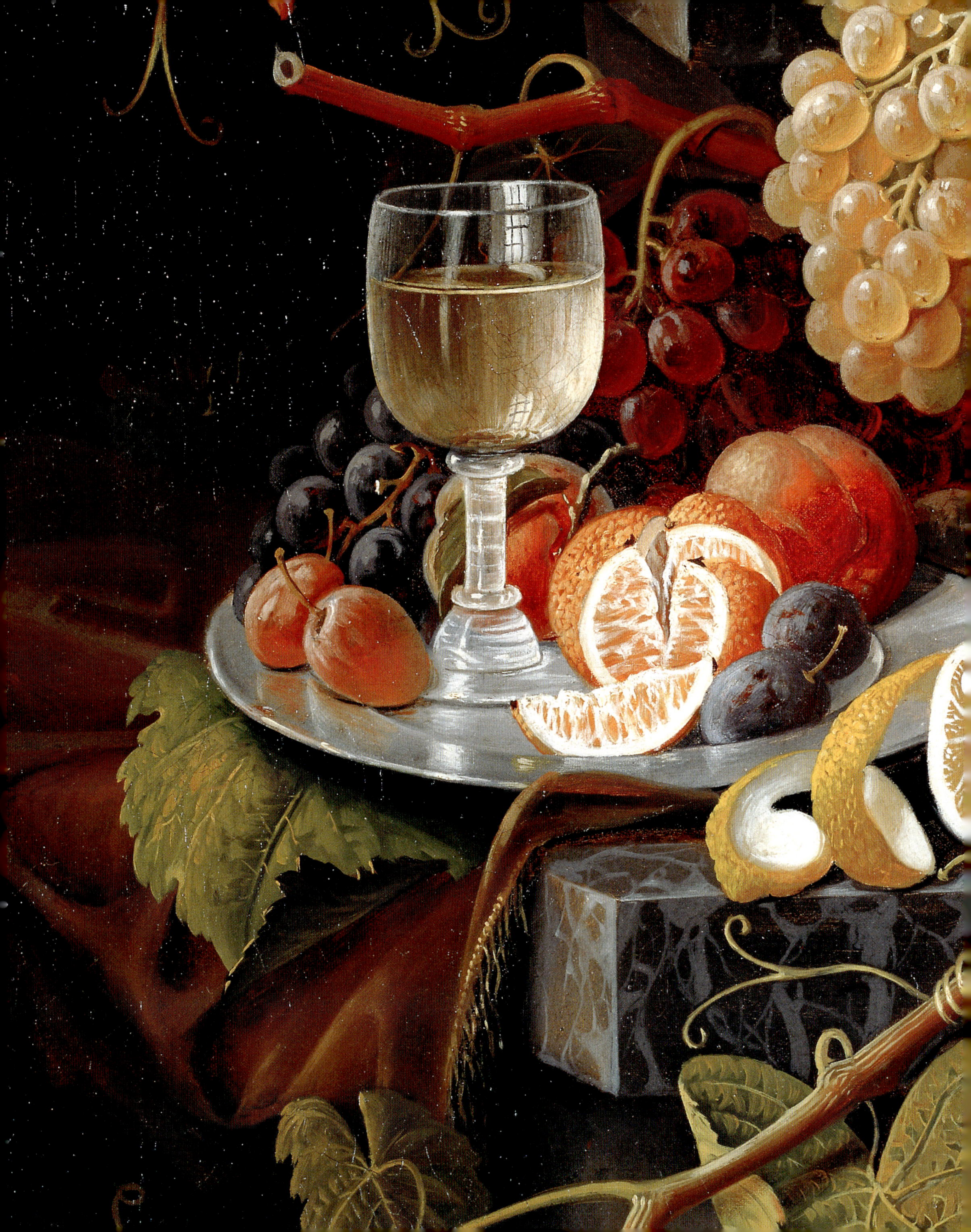

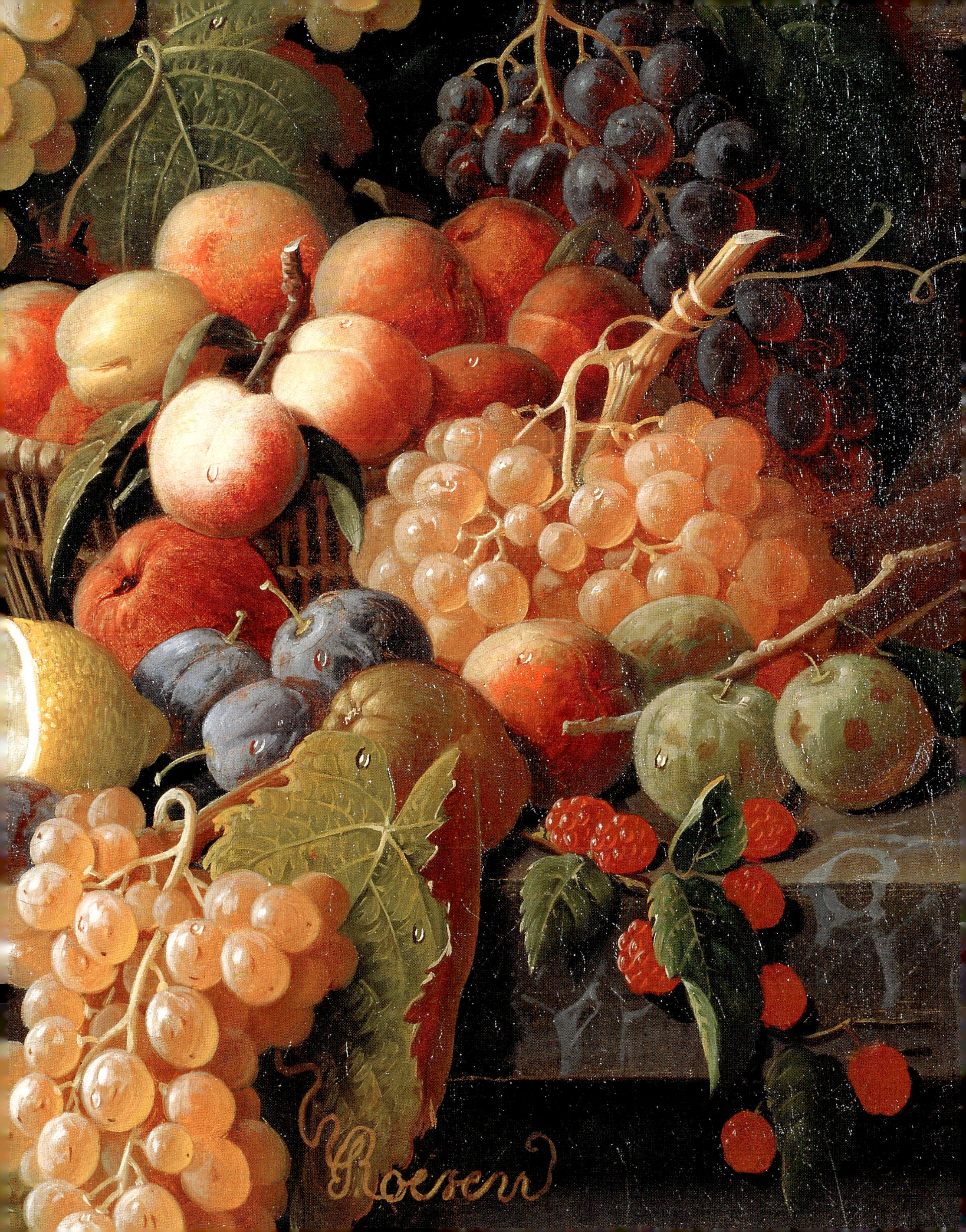
Roesen

# George Hitchcock

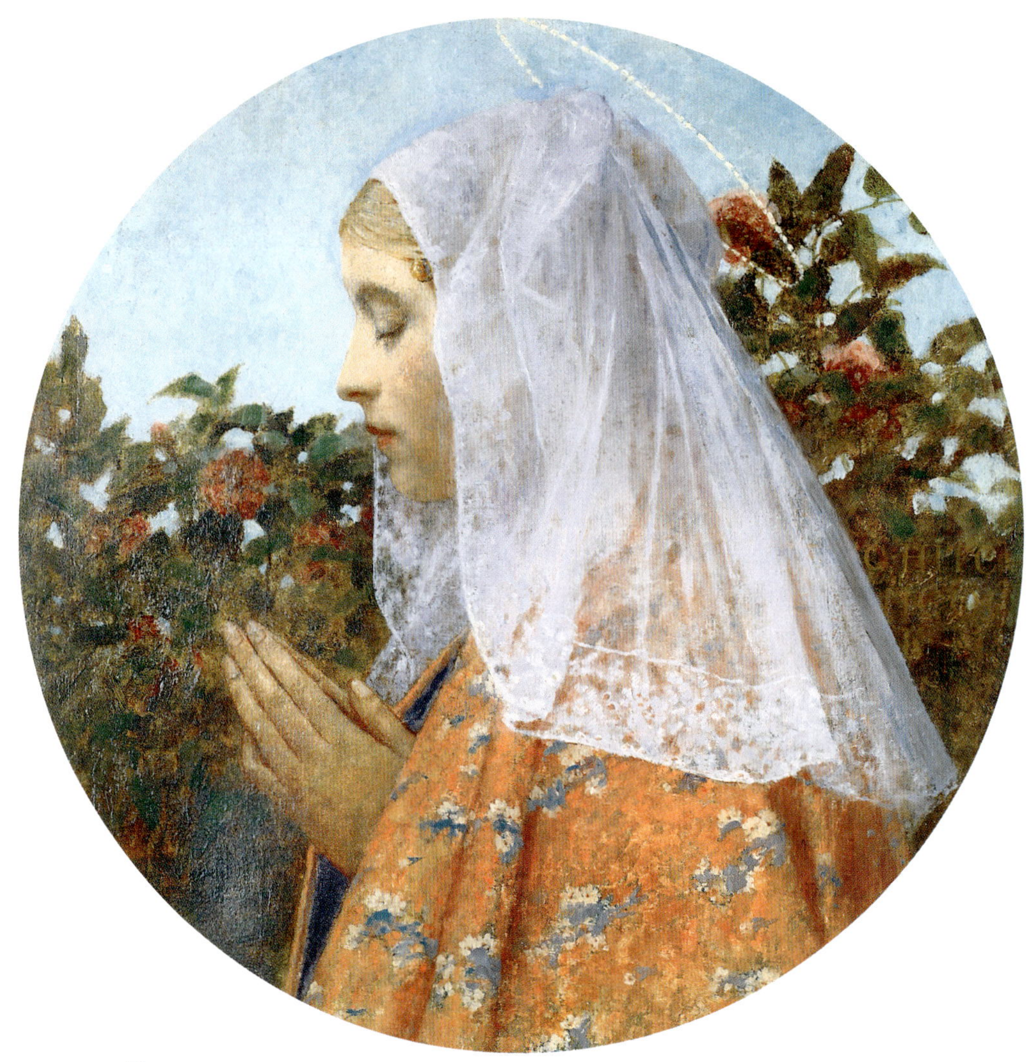

**No. 22**

GEORGE HITCHCOCK (AMERICAN, 1850-1913)
*His Daughter's Wedding Present*
Oil on canvas
24 x 24 inches
Collection of Mr. and Mrs. Fred D. Bentley, Sr.

BORN IN PROVIDENCE, Rhode Island, George Hitchcock attended both Brown University and Harvard and graduated with a law degree in 1874. He quickly abandoned his short-lived law practice for an interest in watercolor and attended Heatherley's School of Fine Art in London. Hitchcock studied with Gustave Boulanger and Jules Lefebvre at the Académie Julian and later studied in Düsseldorf and the Hague. He made his home in Holland, settling in Egmond-aan-Zee, near Amsterdam, where he established a long professional relationship and friendship with fellow artist Gari Melchers. Hitchcock described his adopted homeland as "the most harmonious of all countries, either in sun or shadow. It is never crude; it is always a picture, atmospherically, as it stands, without change or thought of change."[1] Here, he specialized in figure paintings and picturesque landscapes of the coastal town. Many of his paintings, as was fairly common in European paintings in the last quarter of the nineteenth century, were, in fact, religious subjects in the guise of contemporary genre scenes. Labeled the "painter of light," Hitchcock celebrated traditionally picturesque motifs and avoided any reference to the rapidly developing industrial aspect of modern life. Hitchcock's decorative use of Impressionism brought him international success when he exhibited at both the National Academy of Design in New York and at the Paris Salon of 1885. Awarded the Honorable Mention at the Salon of 1887 and the gold medal at the 1889 Exposition Universelle, Hitchcock enjoyed critical and commercial success in America and continued to exhibit in New York, Providence, and Detroit throughout his career.[2]

Both Hitchcock and his colleague Melchers returned to the theme of wedding portraits throughout their careers. *His Daughter's Wedding Present*, however, had special meaning for Hitchcock, who featured his daughter in a tondo portrait reminiscent of Old Master depictions of the Virgin Mary. At the turn of the century, Hitchcock turned increasingly to decorative concerns by placing more emphasis on the relation of colors and the quality of sunlight. His composition is dominated by the quarter-length profile bust of his daughter, wearing a translucent wedding veil and cloaked in a colorful cape. The orange, blue, and white decorative design pays homage to Hitchcock's adopted land of Holland. The halo indicating purity and virginity, the hands joined in prayer, and the pious expression transform the young girl into a fashionable image of the Madonna.

---

1 George Hitchcock, *Scribner's Magazine*, 2 August 1887, 161

2 Biographical material taken from Janice Oresman, "Gari Melchers' Portraits of Mrs. George Hitchcock," *Archives of American Art Journal* 20 (1980): 19-24; Michael Quick, *American Expatriate Painters of the Late Nineteenth Century* (Dayton: The Dayton Art Institute, 1976); and Theodore E. Stebbins, Jr., *A New World: Masterpieces of American Painting 1760- 1910* (Boston: Museum of Fine Arts, 1983), 252.

# William Morris Hunt

As a painter, sculptor, printmaker, art theorist, and teacher, William Morris Hunt embodied the diverse ambitions of American artists working at mid-century. Born into a prominent New England family, Hunt spent his early years studying sculpture with John Crookshanks King in Boston. Seeking further training and respite from the cold winter months, Hunt traveled abroad, where he trained as a sculpture student at the Düsseldorf Academy in 1845. Two years later, he changed his focus to painting and enrolled at Thomas Couture's newly formed atelier in Paris. Couture advocated a return to the technique and subject matter of the Old Masters, which Hunt incorporated into a series of genre paintings that combined modern urban subjects with compositional arrangements and motifs adopted from the Old Masters. He balanced these urban city types with noble depictions of French peasants inspired by the work of Jean-François Millet in nearby Barbizon. Hunt returned to Boston in 1855, eager to share his new-found knowledge. He published a series of lithographs based on his work in France and in Newport, Rhode Island, and opened his own small school there modeled after the French system. Hunt's painterly technique and French subject matter, however, met with resistance from the academic circles in Boston that still embraced the aesthetic of the dominant Hudson River school and the influential theories on nature by John Ruskin. Hunt's work was deemed a "departure from the truth" and "destitute in meaning and sentiment." More traditional portrait painting dominated his oeuvre over the next decade and these works found a large audience among Boston's elite. His intimate depictions of men and women went beyond physiognomic accuracy and explored the psychological and emotional characters of his sitters. At the end of the Civil War, Hunt returned to Paris and accompanied his friend and fellow painter Elihu Vedder on sketching trips to Brittany. Like the Barbizon school painters, Hunt sought to define naturalistically his subject matter using color alone, and his *plein-air* landscapes of this period demonstrate his ease with the new themes and techniques. Upon his return to Boston, he persuaded people to accept Barbizon school paintings. His efforts created a growing movement toward tonal concerns and subjective responses to nature. While the years 1868-72 were difficult ones, marked by personal and professional losses, Hunt's enthusiasm for dark and broadly brushed landscapes by French artists found increasing acceptance among American collectors; by Hunt's death, it was fast becoming the dominant style of American landscape painting.[1]

Following the tragic fire of 1872 in Boston, in which Hunt lost many canvases, he decided to travel along the eastern seaboard. Governor's

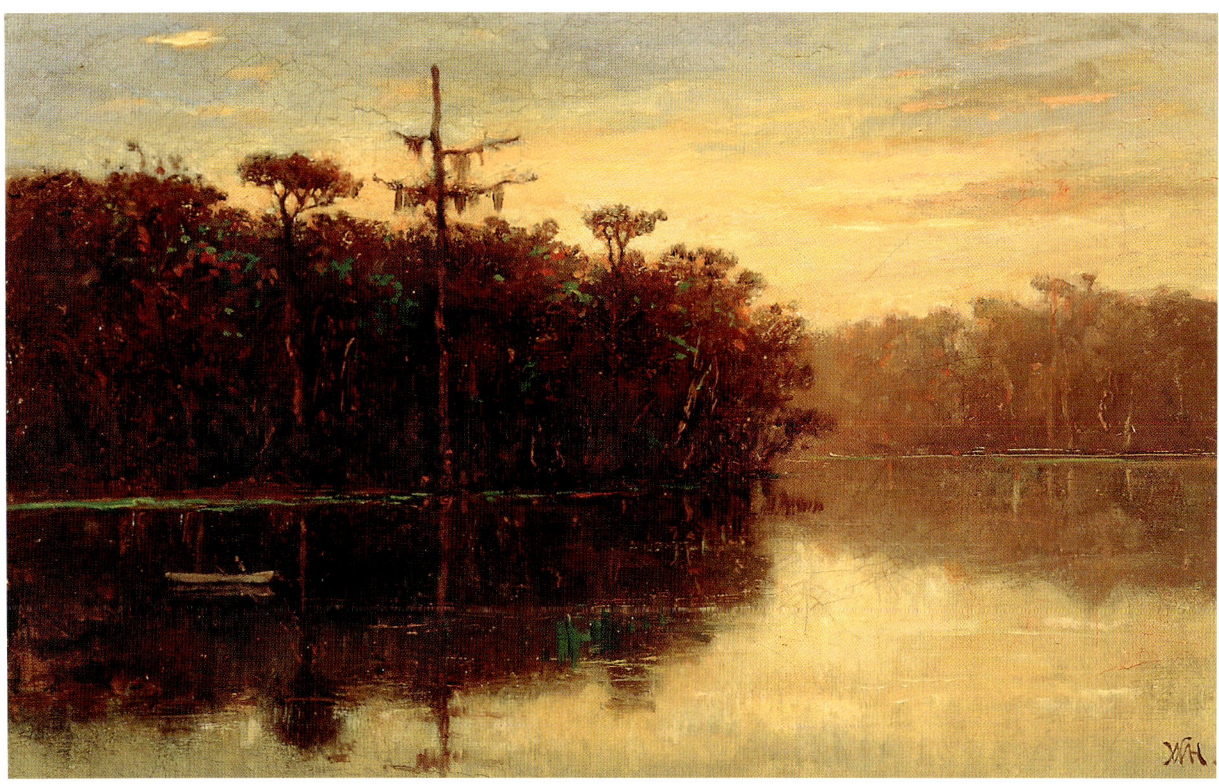

~ **No. 23** ~

William Morris Hunt (American, 1824-1879)
*Governor's Creek, Florida,* 1873-4
Oil on canvas
17 x 24 inches
Collection of the Columbus Museum, Columbus, Georgia

Creek, Florida, a tributary of the Saint Johns River, flows through the once-fashionable spa of Green Cove Springs. Before the advent of railroads, tourists flocked there on steamers from nearby Charleston and Savannah to escape the encroaching industrialization and heal their weary bodies. Hunt celebrated this solitude and peace in *Governor's Creek, Florida*, in which only a sole canoe invades the landscape. Hunt achieves a strong sense of depth with the reflective waters, which wrap around the darkened peninsula in the middle ground and mirror the forest in the distance.

---

1 Biographical information taken from Sharman Wallace McGurn, *The Late Landscapes of William Morris Hunt*, Exhib. cat. (College Park: The University of Maryland Press, 1976); and Sally Webster, *William Morris Hunt, 1824-1879* (Cambridge: Cambridge University Press, 1991).

# Eastman Johnson

Born the son of a politician, Jonathan Eastman Johnson spent his childhood in Fryeburg and Augusta, Maine. His father recognized his natural inclination for drawing and apprenticed him to a Boston lithographer's shop, where he designed title pages for books and music. Finding the work tedious and unimaginative, Johnson returned home and began sketching portraits of his father's political cronies in the state legislature. The aspiring artist joined his family in Washington, D.C., in 1844 and obtained, through his father's contacts, a studio in one of the Senate committee rooms. His sitters included such notable Americans as John Quincy Adams, Mrs. Alexander Hamilton, Dolly Madison, and members of Congress and the Supreme Court. Johnson's desire to continue as a successful portraitist prompted his journey to Europe in 1850. While he initially trained with Emanuel Leutze in Düsseldorf, his exposure to the works of Rembrandt and Van Dyck in the Hague left a lasting impression on his art. Johnson completed his education in Paris under Thomas Couture and returned home to Washington in 1855. He spent the next three years traveling and painting genre scenes and portraits in Wisconsin, Virginia, and Ohio. Eventually, he settled in New York in 1858. With the incredible success of his painting *Negro Life in the South*, exhibited in 1859, the National Academy of Design elected

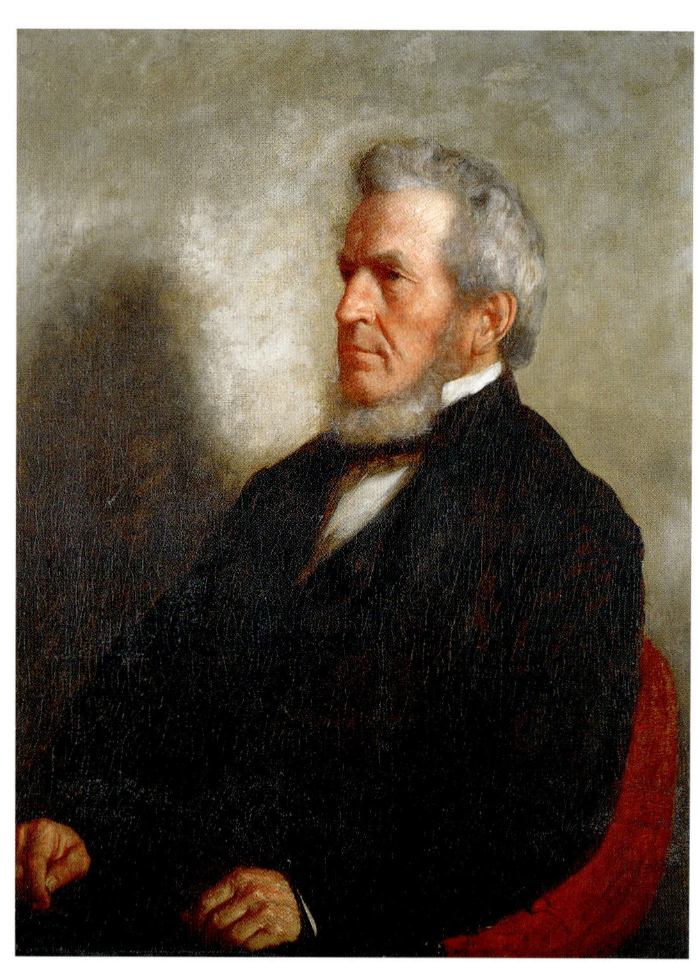

**No. 24**

EASTMAN JOHNSON (AMERICAN, 1824-1906)
*John C. Chandler*, 1860
Oil on canvas
36 x 28 inches
Collection of Mr. and Mrs. Fred D. Bentley, Sr.

Johnson an associate member and gave him full academician status within a year. Over the next two decades, Johnson was devoted to portraying the American scene. His sympathetic Civil War studies, painted at the battle front, and his countless depictions of America's idealized agrarian life established his reputation as one of the country's most poignant storytellers. During these years, however, Johnson never gave up his portrait business, and in 1881, his focus returned to these profitable commissions. His favorite subjects were wealthy New York families and public figures, including John D. Rockefeller, Jay Gould, William H. Vanderbilt, and presidents Grover Cleveland and Benjamin Harrison.[1] Art critic and biographer S.G.W. Benjamin chronicled his appeal in 1882:

> ***. . . although he studied long abroad, he has imported the style of no foreign artists, but has illustrated the principles of art in a manner entirely his own; and because, too, he has been content to look for subjects at home, thus showing himself wholly in sympathy with the attractions of his own land. These qualities have not been characteristic of the work of the new school of American artists, who, while showing ability and enterprise, have purposely imported the styles of Bonnat, Gérôme, Daubigny, Corot, or Manet, together with a selection of subjects entirely foreign and therefore imitative.***[2]

*John C. Chandler* demonstrates Johnson's mastery of oil painting. This composition typifies Johnson's emphasis on the psychological aspect of his sitters. John Chandler, a farmer from Lowell, Maine, was Johnson's uncle. The artist often painted portraits of his family, and his intimate knowledge of their character took visual form in paint. The nondescript, mottled brown background and plain clothing set off Chandler's intelligent visage and capable hands. The hands and head of the man, which symbolized the important joining of intellect and strength, later became a vital aspect of Thomas Eakins's penetrating portraits. Johnson's strong use of chiaroscuro, inspired by the Dutch masters he had studied a decade earlier, along with his selective highlighting and bold modeling of the facial features, adds a sense of drama to the conventional portrait.

---

1 Biographical material taken from John I. H. Bauer, *An American Genre Painter, Eastman Johnson: 1824-1906* (Brooklyn: Brooklyn Institute of Arts and Sciences, 1940); and Patricia Hills, *Eastman Johnson*, Exhib. cat. (New York: C. N. Potter, Inc., 1972).

2 S.G.W. Benjamin, *Magazine of Art* 5 (1882): 490.

# Nell Choate Jones

The daughter of a Confederate Army captain, Nell Choate Jones was born in Hawkinsville, Georgia. In 1884, after her father's death, her family relocated to Brooklyn, New York, where she spent the remainder of her years. In the mid-1920s, with support from her husband, the painter Eugene Jones, she gave up a teaching career to work on her art full-time. Her success was immediate. Jones received critical praise for her impressionistic views of Europe and within two years was awarded a scholarship to study at the art school in Fontainebleau, France. She returned to the South in 1936 for her sister's funeral and found, in spite of her grief, the inspiration for many of her future compositions. Her simplified forms, rhythmic designs, and intense color combined to produce an almost expressionistic sense of nature's latent energies.[1] While her later paintings focused on the rural South, she remained an active member of the Brooklyn art community and served as president for three organizations, including the Brooklyn Society of Artists (1949-52), the American Society of Contemporary Artists (1951-5), and the National Association of Women Artists.[2] Her identity, however, was tied inextricably to the South; as she stated at ninety-eight years of age, "I was born here, I am a Southerner and that's all there is to it."[3]

In *Georgia Red Clay*, the limited but vibrant palette and deliberate brushstrokes create a feeling of monumental energy within this simple composition. Jones placed two massive trees in the foreground that twist upward into the dark, stormy sky. The stability formed by the two dominant verticals is countered by the dramatic curve of the red clay road, which reaches its crescendo at the precarious edge of the cultivated fields. The fiery red of the road and roofs heighten the excitement and emotion within this rural setting. Her thickly painted Post-Impressionist landscapes captured Georgia's rough terrain and the difficulty in making a living in the rural South during the Depression. Her feeling for the land and the hardship of this life continues a tradition that found expression throughout the region following World War I, particularly in the work of southern Regionalist painters such as Charles Shannon and Lamar Dodd.

---

1 Bruce W. Chambers, *Art and Artists of the South: The Robert P. Coggins Collection*, Exhib. cat. (Columbia: University of South Carolina Press, 1984), 143.

2 Biographical information taken from ibid.; and Pennington, *A Southern Collection*, 168.

3 Quoted in "Confederate's Daughter Returns Home for Visit," *Hawkinsville Dispatch & News*, 3 January 1979, quoted in Pennington, 168.

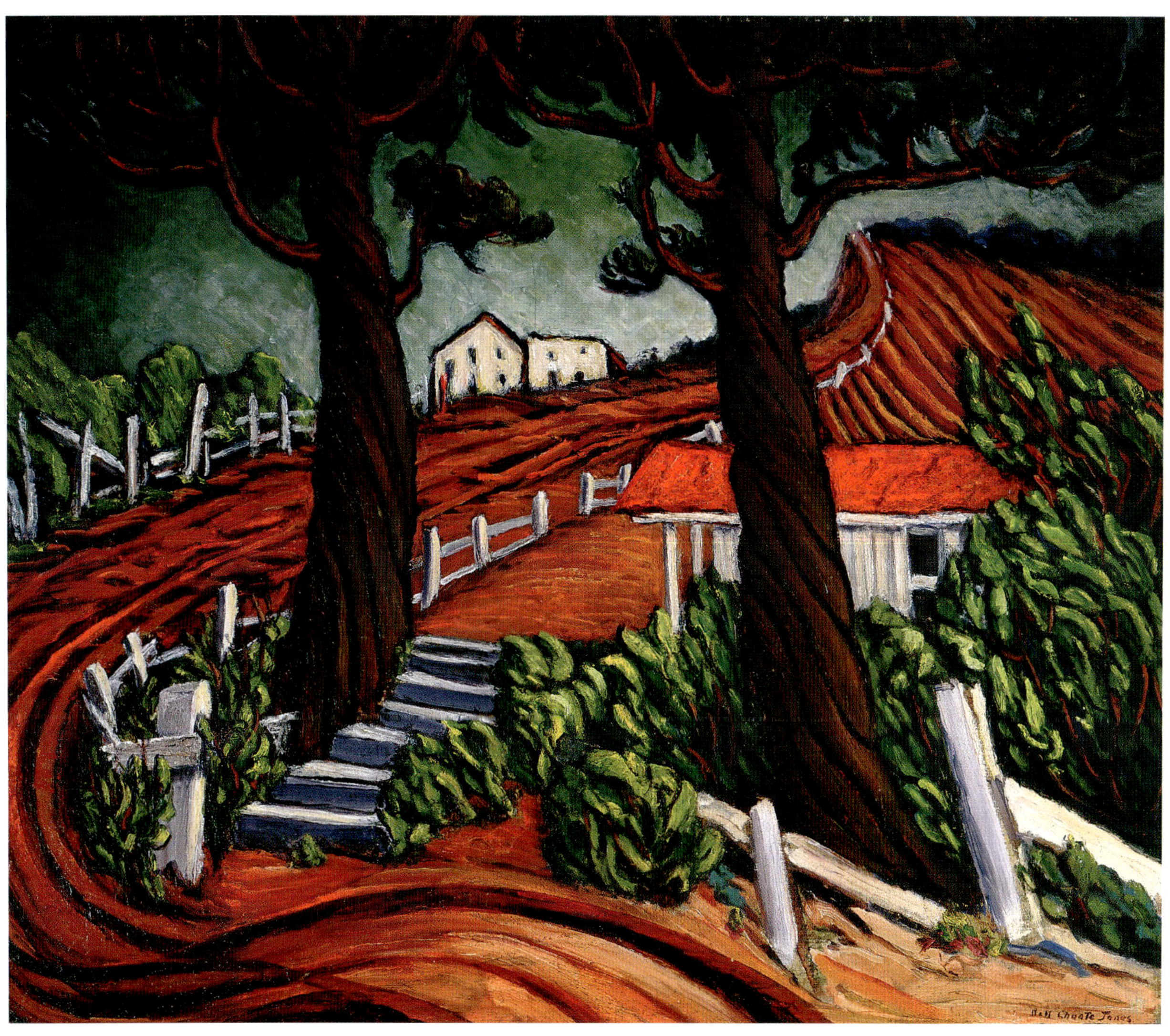

~ **No. 25** ~

Nell Choate Jones (American, 1879-1981)
*Georgia Red Clay*, 1946
Oil on canvas
25 x 30 inches
Morris Museum of Art, Augusta, Georgia

# *Lee Krasner*

Lee Krasner, born Lenore Krassner in Brooklyn, New York, lived for years in the shadow of her famous husband, Jackson Pollock. Today, she is recognized for her vital contributions to New York's first generation of Abstract Expressionists. Her parents, both Russian Jewish immigrants, fled the persecution and poverty of their homeland to a new start in America. While their interests were primarily literary and political, they supported their daughter's decision to become an artist. She began her studies at the Washington Irving High School for Girls, the only secondary school to offer a studio program, and continued her training at the Women's Art School at Cooper Union from 1926 until 1929. Krasner later enrolled at the conservative National Academy of Design, where she received training in drawing, composition, and technique. Her style changed drastically after she viewed exhibitions of Paul Cézanne, Georges Seurat, Vincent van Gogh, and Paul Gauguin at the new Museum of Modern Art. Inspired by the brilliant color and heavily impastoed brushwork of the modernists, Krasner staged a "revolution" at the Academy. Her dissent met with disapproval from her teacher, Social Realist Leon Kroll, who told her to "go home and take a mental bath" after viewing her newly liberated style. Krasner continued to work in a modernist vein under the German painter Hans Hoffman at his newly formed art school in Greenwich Village. During her three years with Hoffman (1937-40), Krasner increasingly manipulated the surface of the picture plane with robust application of paint. She worked within a Cubist idiom derived from Picasso and utilized the brightly colored palette of the Fauves. Krasner's associations with avant-garde art critics Harold Rosenburg and Clement Greenberg and her exposure to the theories of the eccentric Russian émigré John Graham initiated her first investigations of what became Abstract Expressionism in the early 1940s. In 1942, she met her future husband Jackson Pollock, who had successfully captured the raw energy of primitive form in his paintings. Her admiration of his method soon drove her own artistic evolution. Krasner's heavily impastoed Cubist abstractions slowly evolved into the more open, spontaneous style of action painting later in the decade. She set out in a new direction, creating an important series of works known as the "Little Image" paintings, which combined an interest in primitive hieroglyphic forms and the Abstract Expressionist technique of dripping or spilling paint directly on the canvas and letting chance rule the outcome. As Pollock's fame grew, Krasner receded into the background. Continually dissatisfied with her work, Krasner reworked and destroyed many of her paintings. Overlooked by her chauvinist colleagues and slighted by galleries, who labeled her "the artist's wife," Krasner increasingly withdrew from the art scene and devoted herself to Pollock, who was suffering from the accumulated effects of alcoholism and drug abuse. His death in 1956 marked a difficult period for Krasner, whose moody creations reflected her inner torment. By 1965, however, Krasner revived both emotionally and professionally. Her large, brightly colored canvases were included in a major retrospective of her work at the Whitechapel Art Gallery in London. Krasner's retroactive inclusion by scholars and critics in the avant-garde artistic movement Abstract Expressionism righted an historical injustice.[1]

Between 1938 and 1940, Krasner executed a series of figurative charcoals and oil paintings under the tutelage of Hoffman. *Study from Life* represents her rejection of her academic training and her full assimilation of Hoffman's sensibility. The composition becomes a study of both positive and negative space, characterized by heavily impastoed brushstrokes and bright palette. While the figure and some studio elements, including an easel and canvas at the right edge of the composition, are still discernible, it is apparent that Krasner was more interested in the juxtaposition of form and color than the actual studio setting. She worked across the entire surface of the canvas, giving rhythmic value to forms, not in a hierarchical composition, but rather in a free flow with a spatial conception derived from the colors' values.

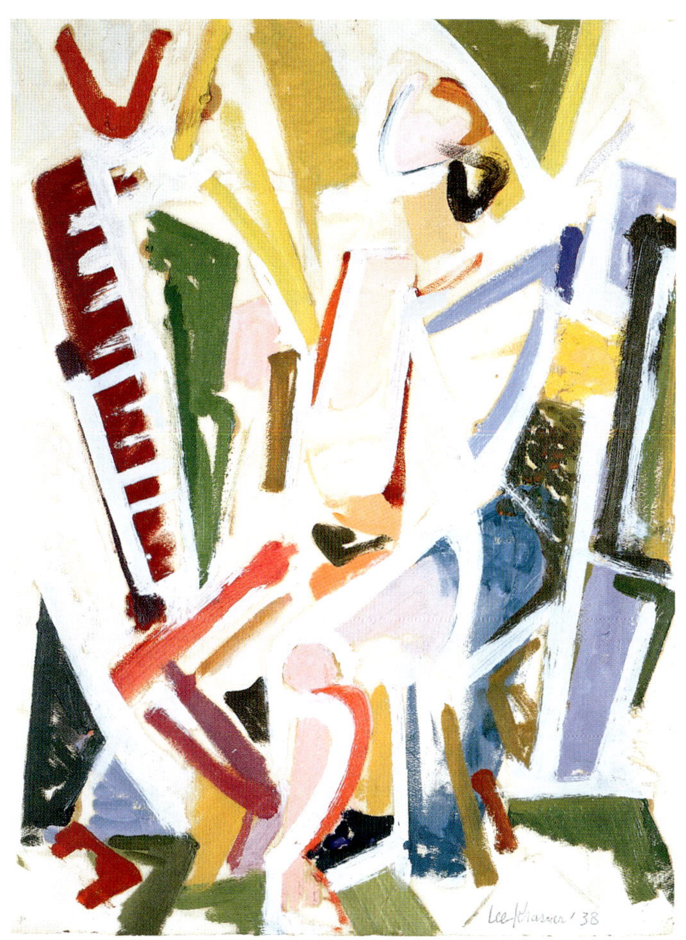


**No. 26**

LEE KRASNER (AMERICAN, 1911-1984)
*Study from Life*, 1938
Oil on paper
24 ¾ x 19 inches
High Museum of Art, Atlanta; purchase, 1979.7


---

1 Biographical information taken from Robert Hobbs, *Lee Krasner* (New York: Abbeville Press, 1993); Ellen J. Landau, *Lee Krasner: A Catalogue Raisonné* (New York: Harry N. Abrams, 1995); and Barbara Rose, *Lee Krasner: A Retrospective*, Exhib. cat. (New York: Museum of Modern Art, 1983).

# Leon Kroll

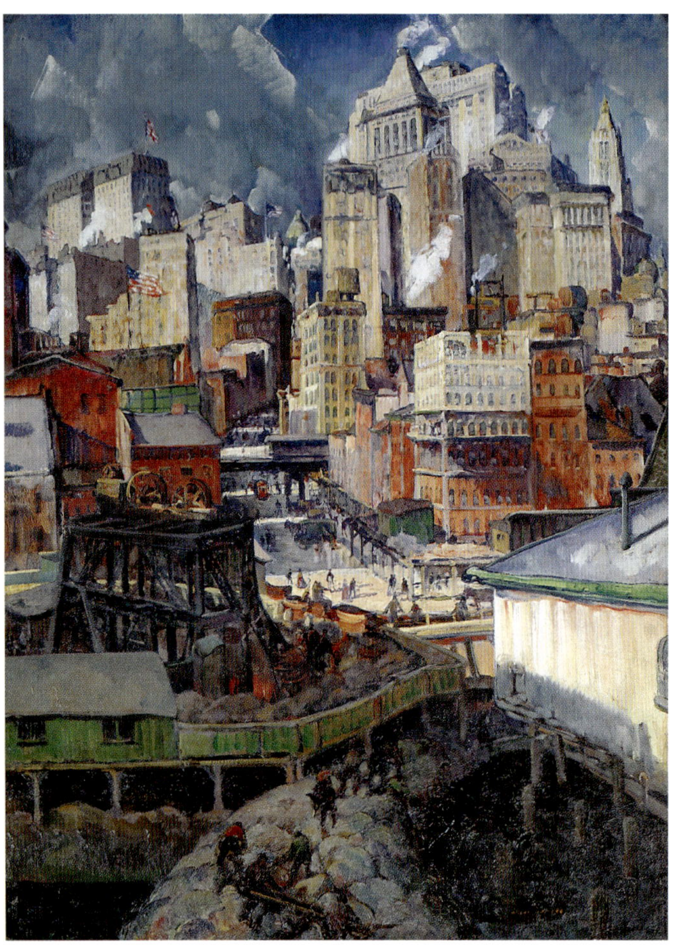

~ **No. 27** ~

LEON KROLL (AMERICAN, 1884-1974)
*Manhattan Rhythms,* ca. 1915
Oil on canvas
48 x 36 inches
Collection of Terry and Margaret Stent

THE CHAOTIC, INDUSTRIAL, urban setting of New York provided the backdrop for Leon Kroll's earliest artistic efforts. Born in the city, Kroll supported himself as a mechanical draftsman for his brother's engineering firm while enrolled at the Art Students League and the National Academy of Design. He received the Mooney scholarship in 1908, which allowed him to study with academic painter Jean-Paul Laurens at the Académie Julian; six months later, Kroll won the coveted Grand Prix award. In Paris, Kroll was introduced to the work of Paul Cézanne and Vincent van Gogh, both of whom had a tremendous impact on his later work. Kroll's growing confidence was bolstered by the critical success of his first one-man show in New York in 1911. A friendship with painter George Bellows assured Kroll entry into the exclusive circle of Social Realist artists centered around members of the disbanded Eight. Even though he was a product of the Academy, the realists Robert Henri, John Sloan, William Glackens, George Luks, Edward Hopper, and Eugene Speicher included Kroll's cityscapes and figure paintings in their exhibitions. In 1913, Kroll was invited to participate in the Armory Show; the exposure he received at this exhibition effectively launched his career. Thereafter, his heavily painted urban scenes were as avidly collected as the Cubist paintings of the European modernists. After another brief stay in Europe, Kroll returned to his teaching position at the National Academy in 1915, where he taught theory and painting for the next two years.

Kroll traveled continually during these years and joined George Bellows and Robert Henri in Santa Fe, New Mexico, where he created works inspired by the southwestern landscape. Specialization in a particular genre never interested the prolific artist, who painted figures, cityscapes, landscapes, and still-lifes throughout his career. Kroll similarly delved into the influential theories of proportion and symmetry proposed by writer-theorist Jay Hambidge and Hardesty Maratta's color studies. The belief in these scientific approaches to art found a responsive audience during and just after World War I, when many artists desired a sense of controlled harmony in place of the country's deteriorated value systems. Science, balanced by the artist's intuition, could raise the human spirit from the disastrous chaos of war.

The 1920s were productive years for Kroll, who balanced a teaching career, an active exhibition schedule, and frequent painting excursions to Europe. Although he was primarily an easel painter, Kroll accepted several major mural commissions in the 1930s and '40s, most notably for the Justice Department in Washington, D.C., and the War Memorial Building in Worcester, Massachusetts. The sweeping trends of American art at mid-century excluded Kroll, who remained an avid realist throughout his life. His commitment to humanity is apparent both in his paintings and in his words: "I sense the 'beyondness,' the wonder, of simple-living people and the things they do. I try to express this feeling without being too obvious about it."[1]

*Manhattan Rhythms* was one of many cityscapes executed *en plein air* by Kroll. The crowded cityscape plays on modern notions of the urban reality of early twentieth-century New York. Kroll consciously juxtaposes the darkened rock quarry, inhabited by an immigrant labor force, with the brilliantly lit skyscrapers dominating the upper half of the composition. Man's technical triumph can be seen in the many soaring skyscrapers, blessed both by the heaven-parting skies and the nation, which bestows flags on their monumental accomplishments, while the darker industrial reality of the city is cast in shadow.

---

1 Biographical material taken from Walter Gutman, "Leon Kroll," *Art in America* 18 (October 1930): 299-303; and Nancy Hale and Fredson Bowers, eds., *Leon Kroll: A Spoken Memoir* (Charlottesville: University Press of Virginia, 1983).

# Ernest Lawson

ERNEST LAWSON, A MEMBER of the second generation of American Impressionists began his studies at the Art Students League in New York. He soon abandoned the conventional techniques promoted at the League in favor of the new Impressionism being taught at the Cos Cob Art School in Connecticut. Formed by John Henry Twachtman and Julian Alden Weir, the school concentrated on impressionistic landscape painting. Lawson continued his studies at the Académie Julian in Paris under Jean-Paul Laurens and Benjamin Constant but soon returned to America to set up residence in Washington Heights, New York, in 1898. Ten years later, Lawson formed a lasting friendship with Robert Henri and the controversial group of realist painters known as the Eight. He exhibited with the group at MacBeth Galleries in New York in 1908 and two years later in the exhibition of Independent Artists. The Eight focused on the darker side of urban life; while Lawson was undoubtedly the most conservative member of the group, he too began to paint images of the poverty-stricken areas of New York. He was a dedicated landscape painter and rarely included human figures in his compositions. The Harlem and East Rivers, the Hudson at Inwood, and the cliffs at Hoboken dominated Lawson's compositions until 1916, when he was awarded the Corcoran Gallery Prize, which enabled him to travel to Spain. His thickly textured surfaces and characteristic colorful palette earned praise from contemporary critics, who referred to Lawson's style as "a palette of crushed jewels." After his return from Spain, Lawson lived and worked in Florida until his death in 1939.[1]

Lawson often worked within a single theme, creating several versions of one scene; *The Pigeon Stealers* is an example of this method. Closely related in composition, technique, and style to one of Lawson's more famous works, *The Pigeon Coop*, of the same year, *The Pigeon Stealers* depicts a winter day along the Harlem River. An excellent example of his "crushed jewel" technique, this work demonstrates Lawson's ability to bring poetic charm to the more sordid elements of New York. While the pigeons are the "prisoners" of the coop, they soar above the poverty of the bleak sheds with a freedom and grace absent from the huddled workers. Lawson's post-impressionistic technique and subject matter separated him from the grittier realism of the Ashcan school, the successors to Henri's circle.

---

1 Biographical material taken from Sidney Berry-Hill and Henry Berry-Hill, *Ernest Lawson, American Impressionist, 1873-1939* (England: Leigh-on-Sea, 1968); and Adeline Lee Karpiscak, *Ernest Lawson, 1873-1939*, Exhib. cat. (Tucson: University of Arizona Museum of Art, 1979).

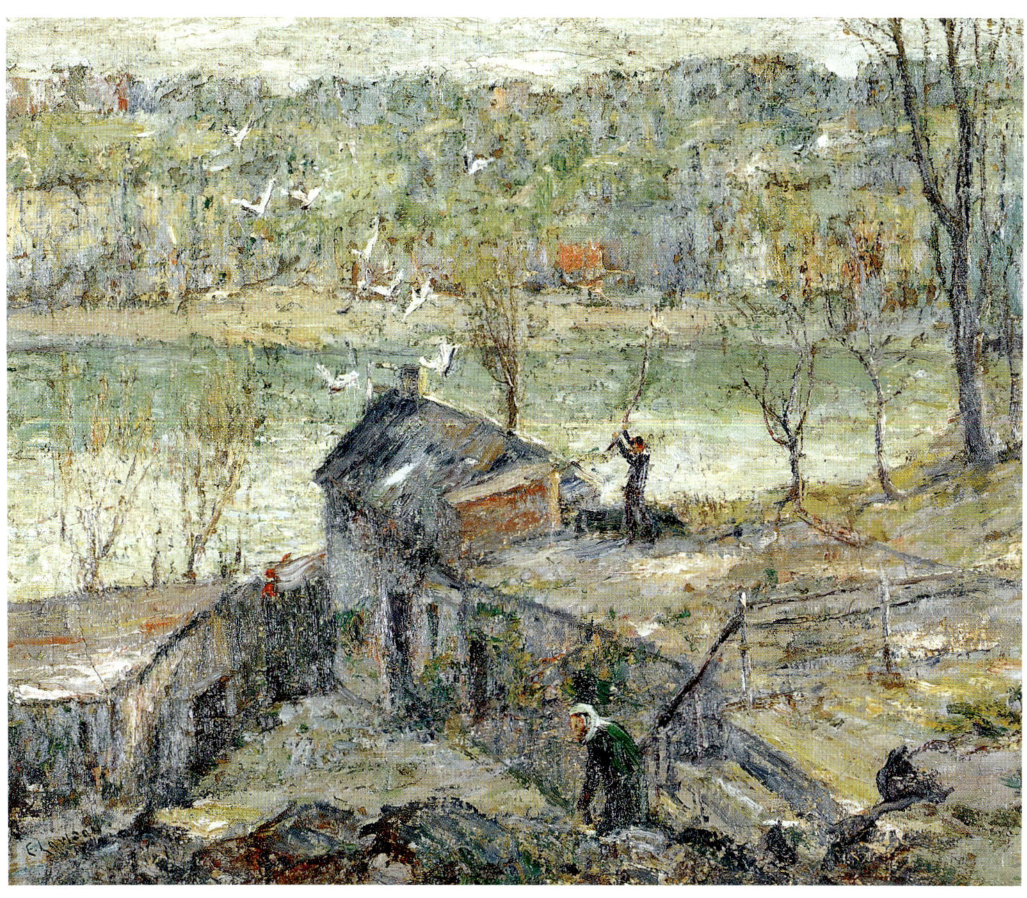

**No. 28**

Ernest Lawson (American, 1873-1939)
*The Pigeon Stealers*, ca. 1916
Oil on canvas
20 x 24 inches
Collection of Stephen and Linda Sessler

# John Marin

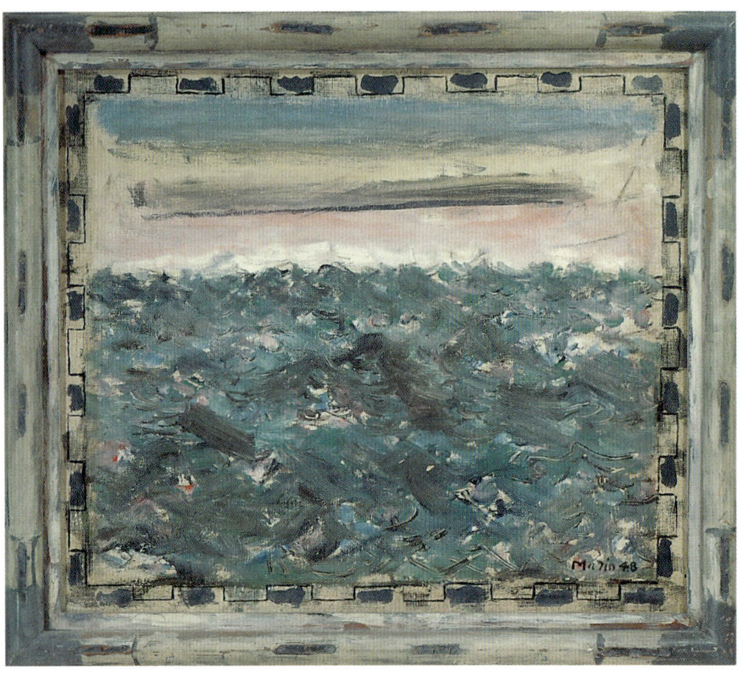

No. 29

JOHN MARIN (AMERICAN, 1870-1953)
*Sea, Light Red and Cerulean Blue*, 1948
Oil on canvas
25 x 30 inches
High Museum of Art, Atlanta
Purchase with bequest of C. Donald Belcher, 1977.48

JOHN MARIN WAS BORN IN RUTHerford, New Jersey, but moved to nearby Weehawken to live with his maternal grandparents after his mother died. He spent his summers fishing and sketching in the mountain ranges of the Catskills and in the wilderness of Minnesota and Wisconsin. He credited his development as an artist to these trips, declaring that he "derived very little" from his years of study at the Pennsylvania Academy of the Fine Arts and the Art Students League.[1] Beginning in 1905, Marin spent five years in Paris and again minimized the impact of his academic exposure, by stating that he ". . . played some billiards, incidently knocked out some batches of etchings." Nevertheless, in Europe, Marin formed a lasting friendship with the American photographer Alfred Stieglitz. In 1909, Stieglitz exhibited Marin's work at his Photo-Secession gallery, known as "291," and propelled his name into New York's circles of modern art. Later, Stieglitz took over the artist's financial affairs and gave him complete freedom to work. Revitalized, Marin returned to New York in 1911 and focused on the city's new architectural monuments as his principal subjects. He captured the energy of the city and depicted in his paintings of the newly built Woolworth Building, the Municipal Building, and the Brooklyn Bridge the basic structural powers, or "pull forces," that he experienced and admired. In 1914, Marin married and settled in Cliffside,

New Jersey. He sought in nature an energy equal to that of the city and found it eventually in the dramatic scenery of Maine's rugged coast. The essential forces of the state's islands dominated his otherwise restrained canvases. He achieved what he termed a "Blessed Equilibrium" within his work by maintaining a structured spatial order and by limiting both his palette and number of brushstrokes. Within this contained equilibrium, however, Marin created frantic paintings of the ocean. "Movement," "forces," and "disorder," were to be contained within the "boundaries" of the canvas. Marin's effort to remain true to his subject was matched by his desire to remain true to the essence of his medium; hence, one is always conscious of the flatness of the surface and the differing effects of the paint. His powerful manipulation of oil and watercolor is evident in his ability to attain a level of translucence in oil and viscosity in watercolor.

During the 1930s and '40s, Marin developed fully as a painter of the sea. Reminiscent of the musically titled compositions by Whistler and Wassily Kandinsky, Marin referred to his pictures as "Movements," and created compositions devoid of human presence. "Here the sea is so damned insistent," he stated, " that houses and land things won't appear much in my pictures." Cubism and Expressionism are reflected within his oeuvre, yet Marin always maintained an independent spirit and loyalty only to himself and his subjects.[2]

*Sea, Light Red and Cerulean Blue* captures the movement and rhythmic vitality of the sea and sky. Marin employed broad brushstrokes of clouds which, in their translucency, reveal much of the canvas underneath; he reasserted the weight of the oil paint, however, in the darkened waves of the ocean. The painted frame and interior decorative border serve to unite frame and picture into one harmonious vision while establishing a tension between the picture plane, frame, and the space behind the picture plane. In the 1930s and '40s Marin often utilized these devices to flatten the three-dimensionality of the nature that he so energized with his brushstrokes. The simplistic interior border contains the seascape, yet never threatens to break Marin's beloved two-dimensional field or subdue nature's energy. While quite different from other members of Stieglitz's circle, in particular Arthur Dove, he found much the same dynamism in nature's forms as Dove did.

---

1 All artist statements quoted in Larry Curry, *John Marin: 1870-1953*, Exhib. cat. (Los Angeles: Los Angeles County Museum of Art, 1970).

2 Biographical material taken from Curry; Cleve Gray, ed., *John Marin by John Marin* (New York: Holt, Rinehart & Winston, undated); MacKinley Helm, *John Marin*, with a foreword by John Marin (Boston: Pellegrini & Cudahy, 1948); and Klaus Kertess, *Marin in Oil*, Exhib. cat. (South Hampton: The Parrish Art Museum, 1987).

# *Alfred Maurer*

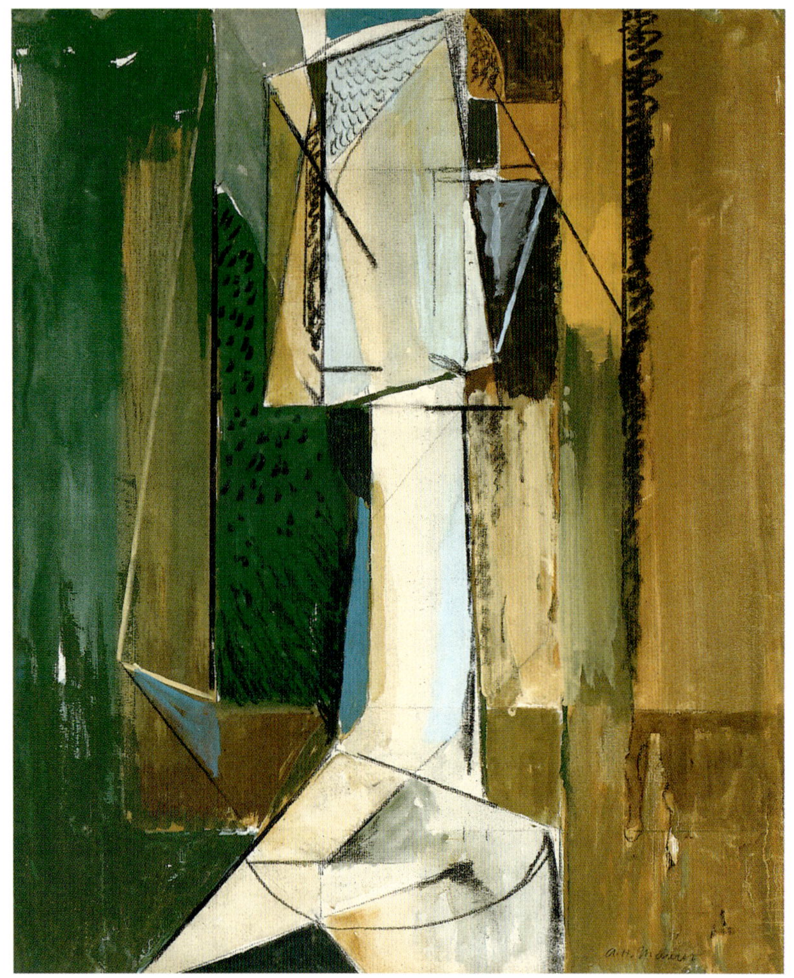

**No. 30**

Alfred Maurer (American, 1868-1932)
*Head*, ca. 1930
Gouache on paper
27 x 17 ⅛ inches
High Museum of Art, Atlanta
Purchase with bequest of C. Donald Belcher, 1977.47

Alfred Maurer was one of America's first painters to combine the concerns of the Fauves and Cubists into strikingly modern compositions. He was raised in New York by his father, Louis Maurer, a successful lithographer for Currier and Ives and a conservative genre painter. After several years at the National Academy of Design, Maurer went to Paris and enrolled at the Académie Julian in 1897. He created academic paintings of single female figures in decorative settings and genre scenes of café society. Critical success followed in the form of numerous awards and honors, including first prize at the Carnegie International exhibition in 1901, a gold medal at the International Exposition in Munich in 1905, and a bronze medal at the Pan-American Exposition in 1915. While in Paris, he was introduced to the salon of Gertrude Stein at 27 rue de Fleurus. The artists he met there drastically changed his style and began his transformation into one of America's young revolutionary modernists. Stein hosted painters Pablo Picasso and Henri Matisse, whose Fauvist compositions, full of vibrant color and raw expression, encouraged Maurer to develop a style with a similar sense of freedom. In 1910, he exhibited at Alfred Stieglitz's Photo-Secession gallery, "291," a year after Matisse; three years later, he enjoyed success at the Armory Show. After the outbreak of World War I, Maurer was forced to return to America, where he joined artists Arthur Dove, John Marin, Max Weber, Marsden Hartley, and Patrick Henry Bruce in Stieglitz's circle. While their work was judged too "modern" by American critics, it was dismissed by Europeans as unoriginal and imitative. Poverty forced Maurer to move in with his father, whose contempt for anything other than realism created a deep rift in their relationship. By the end of the war, Maurer was painting in a Cubist manner and creating enigmatic studies of heads and table-top still-lifes. These stylized heads were his final, most personal contribution to modernism. After a career of professional neglect, Maurer committed suicide a few weeks after his father's death in 1932, ironically on the anniversary of the outbreak of World War I.[1]

Maurer's examination of the theme of the head dominated his work after 1920. A modified naturalism characterized the earliest of these, but in 1926 he began to incorporate greater abstraction into his studies. *Head*, executed during the last years of his life, shows his final treatment of the motif. The head has been broken down into fragmented planes, yet still it adheres to Maurer's general compositional arrangement of a human bust placed against an abstracted background. A limited palette of deep green, muddy brown, black, off-white, and teal define the patterned and textured planes and convey, in their even tonality, the depressed emotional state of the artist. The work is a good demonstration of the lasting effects of Picasso's Cubism and the elongated figures created by the Italian Modernist Amedeo Modigliani.

---

1 Biographical information taken from *Alfred H. Maurer, 1868-1932*, Exhib. cat. (Washington, D.C.: National Collection of Fine Arts, 1973); Katherine Kaplan, "Modernist Expressions: Alfred Maurer Heads, 1920-1932," Exhib. brochure (New York: Kraushaar Galleries, 1998); and Elizabeth McCausland, *A. H. Maurer* (New York: Walker Art Center, 1951).

# *Gari Melchers*

GARI MELCHERS, THE SON of Julius Melchers, a professional wood-carver from Germany, grew up in Detroit. Julius encouraged his son's early artistic aspirations and sent him to train at the Royal Academy of Art in Düsseldorf under Karl von Gebhardt and Peter Janssen. Melchers continued his studies with Jules Lefebvre and Gustave Boulanger, in Paris at the Académie Julian, where he met George Hitchcock, a fellow expatriate. Less than a year later, Melchers exhibited *The Letter* at the Ecole des Beaux-Arts in 1892 and earned critical praise for his "plain, finished, picturesque idea . . . admirably drawn and excellently painted." [1] He joined Hitchcock in Egmond-aan-Zee, Holland, in 1884, and began to fill his compositions with Dutch peasants and picturesque landscapes. During the 1890s, his paintings became increasingly decorative in nature. Dutch women cloaked in elaborately wrought costumes were a staple; themes of domestic harmony and tranquility, often with religious overtones, characterized his paintings. While he continued working in Holland into the new century, his subject matter began to shift away from consciously Dutch depictions toward more universal renderings of women in domestic interiors. Reminiscent of the Boston school artists William Paxton and Philip Leslie Hale, Melchers depicted upper-class, cosmopolitan women as decorative objects within equally decorative interiors. Melchers and his wife Corinne moved to Virginia in 1915, but returned to Holland for brief visits in 1922, 1930, and 1932.[2]

*The Unpretentious Garden*, begun the year of Melchers's marriage, was executed at the artist's new studio in Egmond-aan-Zee. The bright palette, overall pattern of brushstrokes, and high-keyed color suggest Melchers's exposure to Impressionism; however, his academic training gives solid form to the architectural elements, which assert their material presence in the background. The springtime scene of domestic harmony reflects Melchers's own happiness at his recent nuptials, which occurred late in his life. Corinne is pictured at left, barely discernible against the flowery foreground. Her lack of definition underscores the age-old association of woman and nature. The presence of the maid in the background suggests the couple's rising social status and economic security.

---

1 "The Great Exhibit: Various Paintings by Detroit Artists Spoken of," *Detroit Free Press*, 13 September 1883, 4, quoted in Diane Lesko, *Gari Melchers: A Retrospective Exhibition*, Exhib. cat. (St Petersburg, Florida: Museum of Fine Arts, 1990), 52.

2 Biographical information taken from ibid.; Janice Oresman, "Gari Melchers' Portraits of Mrs. George Hitchcock," *Archives of American Art Journal* 20 (1980): 19-24; and Michael Quick, *American Expatriate Painters of the Late Nineteenth Century*.

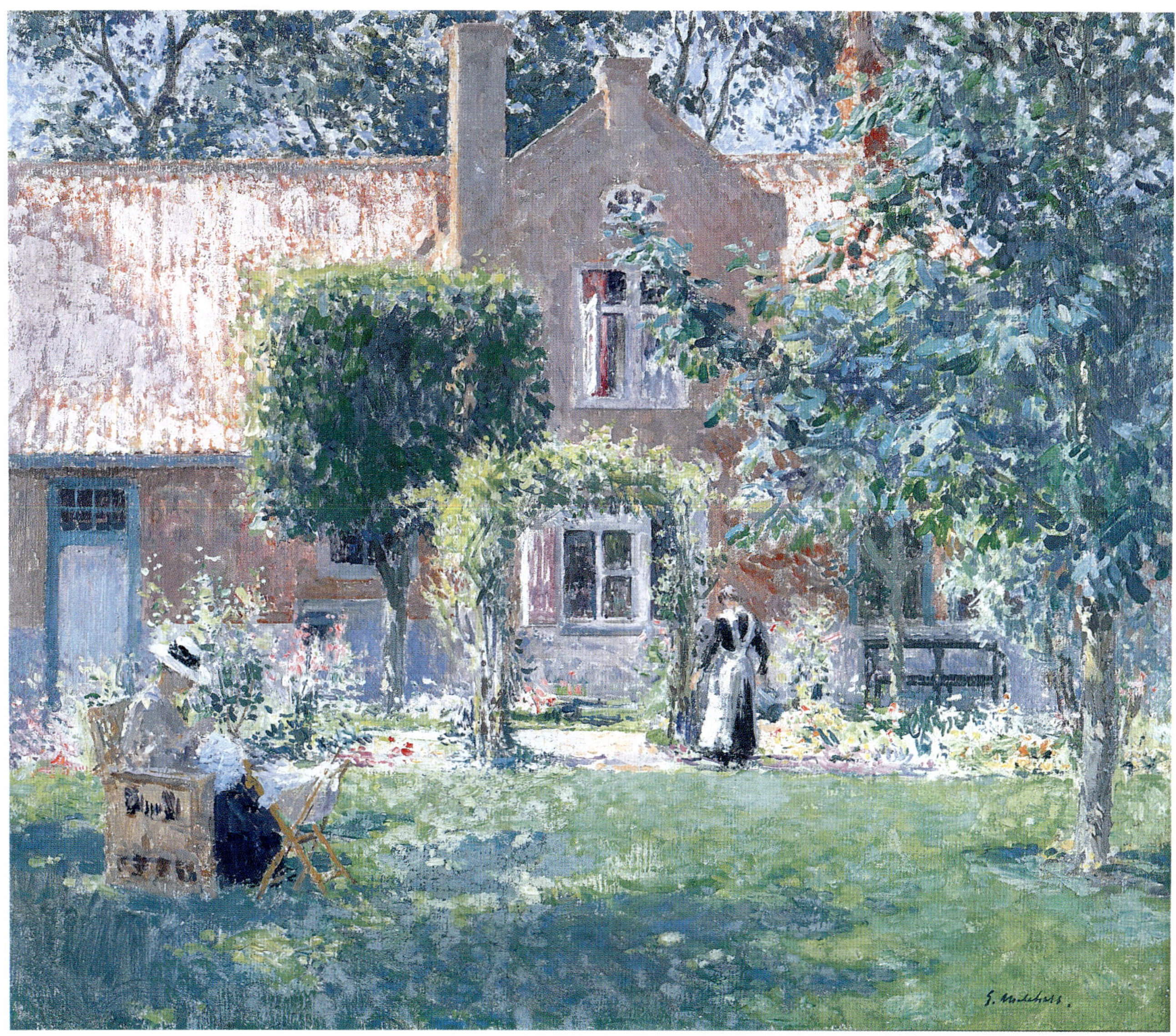

~ **No. 31** ~

GARI MELCHERS (AMERICAN, 1860-1932)
*The Unpretentious Garden*, 1903-09
Oil on canvas
33 ¾ x 40 ¼ inches
Telfair Museum of Art, Savannah, Georgia

# Thomas Moran

At the age of seven, Thomas Moran sailed to America from his native England. In Philadelphia, he served a three-year apprenticeship as an assistant in a wood engraving shop, where he developed his skill as a draftsman. Moran relied on this marketable experience throughout his long career and completed numerous illustrations to augment his income. He returned to England in 1861 to study the Romantic landscapes by J.M.W. Turner and John Constable. Moran retraced Turner's steps along the southern coast of England and sketched *en plein air* in a number of Turner's favorite haunts. In 1866, he journeyed to Paris and Rome; a year later, he enjoyed critical success at the Paris Exposition Universelle, where he was one of a select group of Americans asked to participate. When he returned to America, Moran turned again to illustration and created a number of small engravings of rural Pennsylvania. In 1870, Richard Watson Gilder commissioned Moran to rework a number of field sketches that were to accompany the article "The Wonders of the Yellowstone," by Nathaniel Langford. Having never seen the West, Moran relied on the descriptive article and his own imagination to create a set of drawings that were transformed into wood engravings. Determined to see the land he had only imagined, Moran obtained private funding to travel with Ferdinand Vandeveer Hayden, a geologist who was planning a summer expedition to Yellowstone. Moran had seen the effect of such trips on the work of earlier painters, notably Albert Bierstadt's paintings of the Rocky Mountains, and hoped that his travels would bring him equal fame and money. Hayden's party also included the photographer William Henry Jackson, who intended to document the major monuments of Yellowstone. When the party returned to the East, Hayden used Moran's drawings to argue for Yellowstone's designation as a national park. In 1873, the artist again traveled west, this time as part of Major John Wesley Powell's expedition to explore the Grand Canyon. His final trip in 1892 was funded in part by the Santa Fe Railroad, which used his images as advertisements to entice easterners to journey west. Before he returned home, Moran joined Jackson at the Mammoth Hot Springs Hotel, where he made drawings for Wyoming's state exhibit at the upcoming World's Columbian Exposition in Chicago. He moved to Newark, New Jersey, and set up a studio, where he completed many of the sketches from his travels.[1]

In 1871, Moran arrived in Green River, Wyoming, and executed his "first sketch of the West." Although a town had been established among the striated buttes named Citadel and Castle Rocks, no indication of white settlements ever appeared in Moran's paintings. *Green River* is one of a series intended for eastern viewers and fits their idealization of the West as unspoiled nature. Painted in hues of orange, lavender, and pink, the butte rises high above the Green River, casting its shadow over the small party of Native Americans traveling peacefully through the water. The fantastic coloring and picturesquely appealing Native Americans on horseback were, in fact, creations of Moran's imagination, added later in his New York studio.[2] The far less attractive truth about the region was found in the railroads that crossed through the high-plain deserts of Wyoming and disrupted the natural purity of the land. The rough life of settlers and near extermination of indigenous tribes had no place in Moran's idyllic settings.

1 Biographical material taken from Nancy K. Anderson, *Thomas Moran* (Washington, D.C.: National Gallery of Art, 1997); and *Splendors of the American West: Thomas Moran's Art of the Grand Canyon and Yellowstone*, Exhib. cat. (Birmingham: Birmingham Museum of Art, 1990).

2 Ibid., 49.

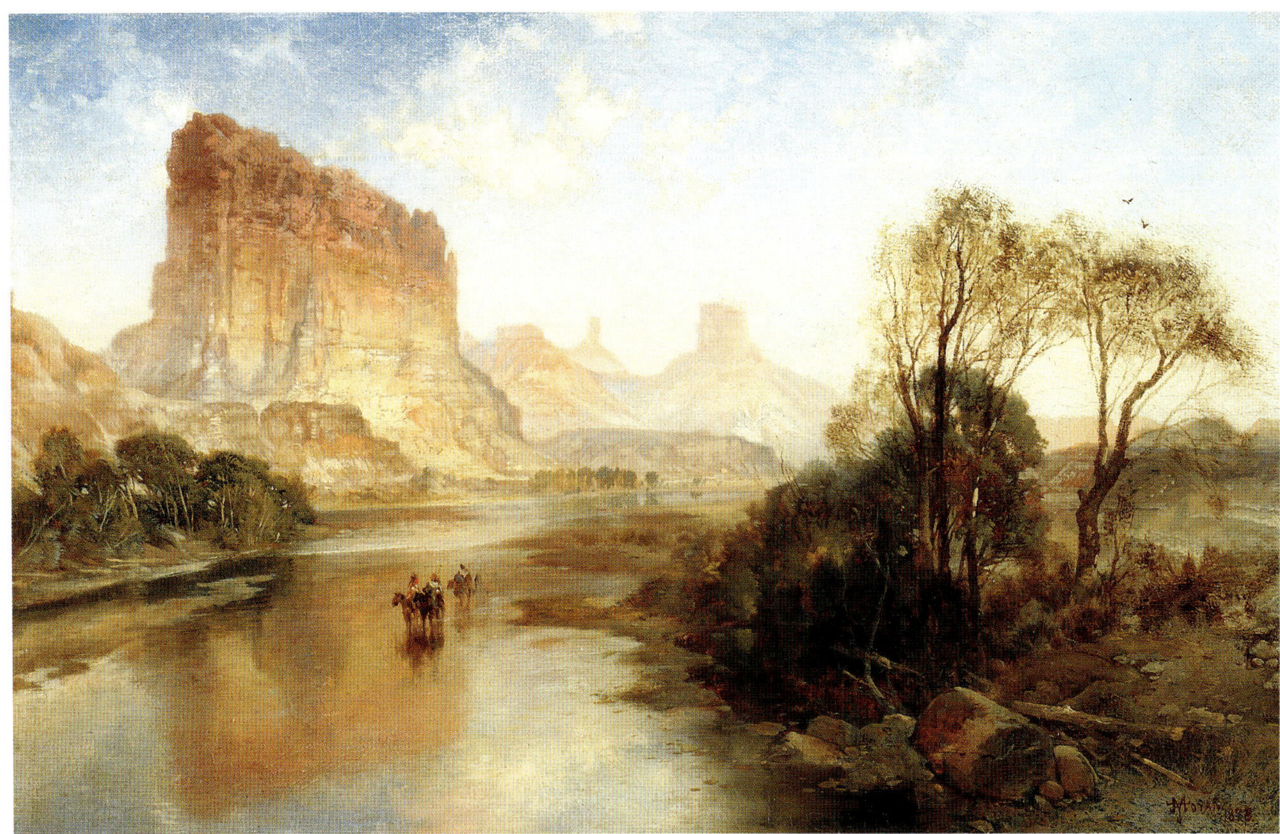

**No. 32**

THOMAS MORAN (AMERICAN, 1837-1926)
*Green River*, 1878
Oil on canvas
36 x 48 inches
Collection of Terry and Margaret Stent

# Robert Emmett Owen

At nineteen, Robert Owen exhibited his work in his hometown of North Adams, Massachusetts, but within a year he left for Boston and enrolled at the Eric Pape School of Art. He earned a steady income as an illustrator for local magazines and newspapers. Owen moved to New York in 1901, where he worked for such prestigious publications as *Scribner's*, *Harper's*, and *Century Magazine*. During his nine years in New York, Owen attended the Art Students League, the Chase School, and the National Academy of Design. By 1910, the artist had relocated to Stamford, Connecticut, and within ten years had opened his own gallery in New York, called the Robert Owen New England Landscape Gallery. While he was a successful artist catering to numerous private clients, his work and name have drifted into anonymity since the 1950s. His lack of involvement within a group, his quiet themes, and his sentimental and traditional approach may possibly account for the dearth of published material on him.[1]

The quiet, agrarian way of life celebrated in *New England Winter, Farm Scene* demonstrates Owen's Impressionist training. The influence of Childe Hassam, Willard Metcalf, and J. Alden Weir, who all worked in New England at the turn of the century, is evident in Owen's bright palette and broad brushstrokes. Winter became a popular motif in many late Impressionist compositions. Twachtman commented upon the poetic nature of winter in a letter to J. Alden Weir, "We must have snow and lots of it. Never is nature more lovely than when it is snowing. Everything is so quiet and the whole earth seems wrapped in a mantle . . . . All nature is hushed to silence."[2] Owen adopted Twachtman's and Weir's penchant for contemplative landscapes without narrative or figures. Numerous painters working in New England, including Metcalf, A.T. Hibbard, and later Eric Sloane, were drawn to the quiet of winter and the pastoral ideals of a bygone era.

---

1 Biographical material taken from Keyes, *American Impressionism in Georgia Collections*, 82.

2 John Twachtman to J. Alden Weir, 16 December 1891, quoted in Gerdts, *American Impressionism*, 159.

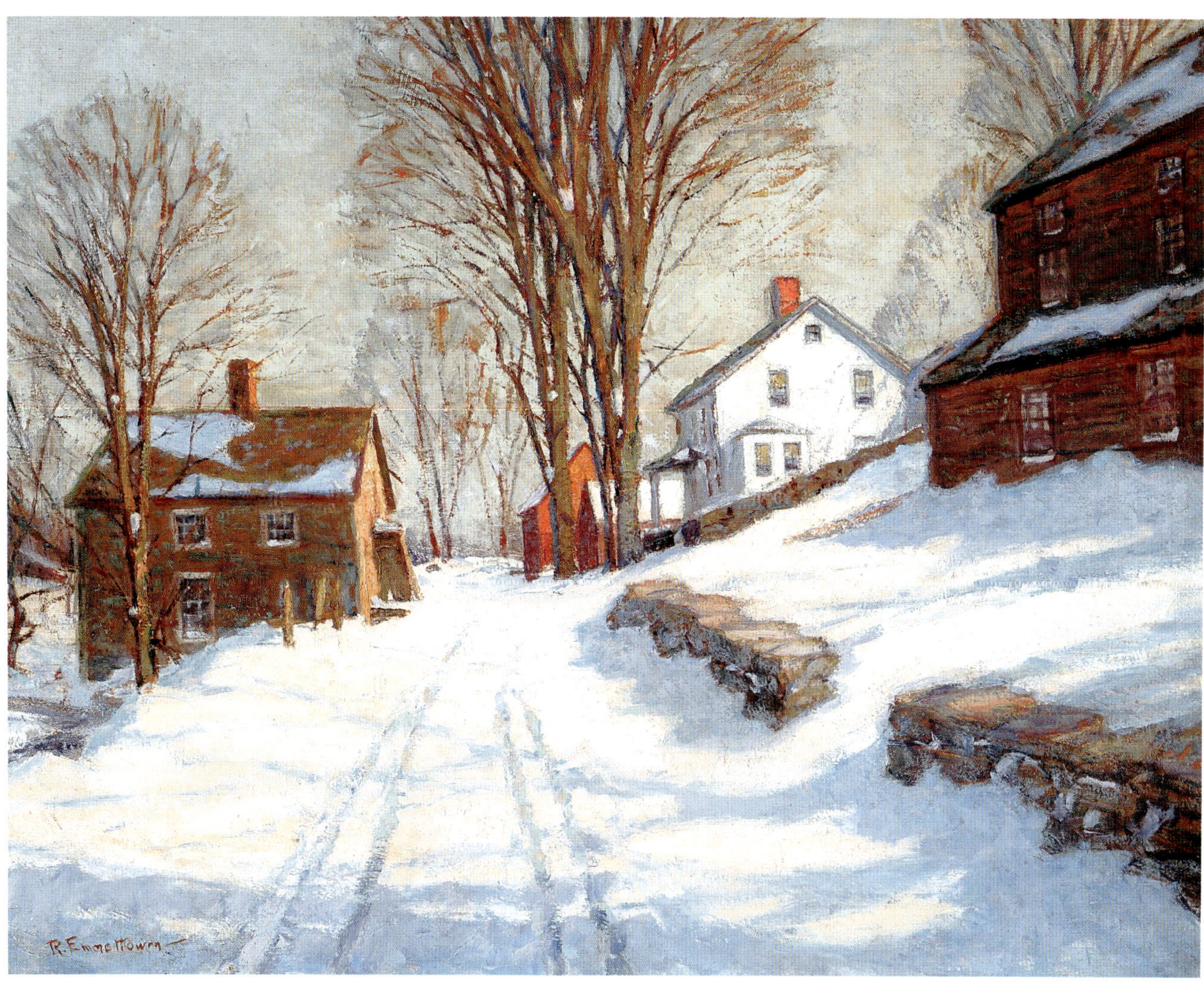

**No. 33**

Robert Emmett Owen (American, 1878-1951)
*New England Winter, Farm Scene,* ca. 1920
Oil on canvas
36 ¼ x 45 inches
Collection of Mr. and Mrs. David E. Miller, Jr.

# William Paxton

William Paxton grew up within the bustling, though conservative, art scene of Boston in the 1870s. He began his studies with Dennis Bunker at the Cowles School of Art in Boston and continued to train at the Académie Julian in Paris. Under the guidance of Jean-Léon Gérôme, Paxton became an able academic figure painter with a firm understanding of shape and form. He returned to the Cowles School in 1893 and worked with Joseph De Camp, the most conservative member of the American Impressionist circle. Paxton's early compositions, executed in the seaside communities of Provincetown and East Gloucester, reflect his active involvement with the Impressionist aesthetic. Young women at leisure blend into brightly lit *plein-air* landscapes. As he moved his subjects indoors to the drawing rooms of upper-class homes, his delicate draftsmanship reasserted itself. De Camp's influence is evident in Paxton's increasingly solid rendering of women, usually alone reading, writing, or admiring jewelry. This theme recalls the work of seventeenth-century Dutch artist Johannes Vermeer, who painted similar scenes of lone female figures in naturally lit interiors. By the twentieth century, however, the popular theme of the young socialite without occupation took on greater social implications. These tranquil domestic interiors were, in effect, an attempt by painters to reestablish the comfortable social hierarchy that existed during the ante-bellum years.[1] The growing suffragette movement in Boston was working to assert women as an important, vital, and intelligent element of society. On the other hand, Paxton's paintings seem to insist that women be admired in the same way as the bric-a-brac decorating their homes. His popularity never waned, however, and visitors continually elected his works as the best at exhibitions.[2]

*The Album* is typical of Paxton's domestic interiors. Probably executed around 1913, the date of the artist's famous painting *The Front Parlor* (St. Louis Art Museum), *The Album* depicts the same interior and model. In this work, she sits straight-backed in a wooden chair and admires a family album of tintype portraits. Her proper posture, delicate features, expensive dress, and genteel activity imply her high social position. Paxton carefully coordinated her rich, emerald green dress and hat with the wallpaper design, at once uniting the composition and confining the model within her setting.

---

1 Bernice Kramer Leader, "Antifeminism in Paintings of the Boston School," *Arts* 1 (1980): 112-19; and Gerdts, *American Impressionism*, 212.

2 Helen Earle noted that *Woman Sewing* and *Girl Arranging Flowers* both won "popular prizes" at the annual exhibitions in Detroit in 1923, *Biographical Sketches of American Artists* (Michigan State Library, 1924), 243.

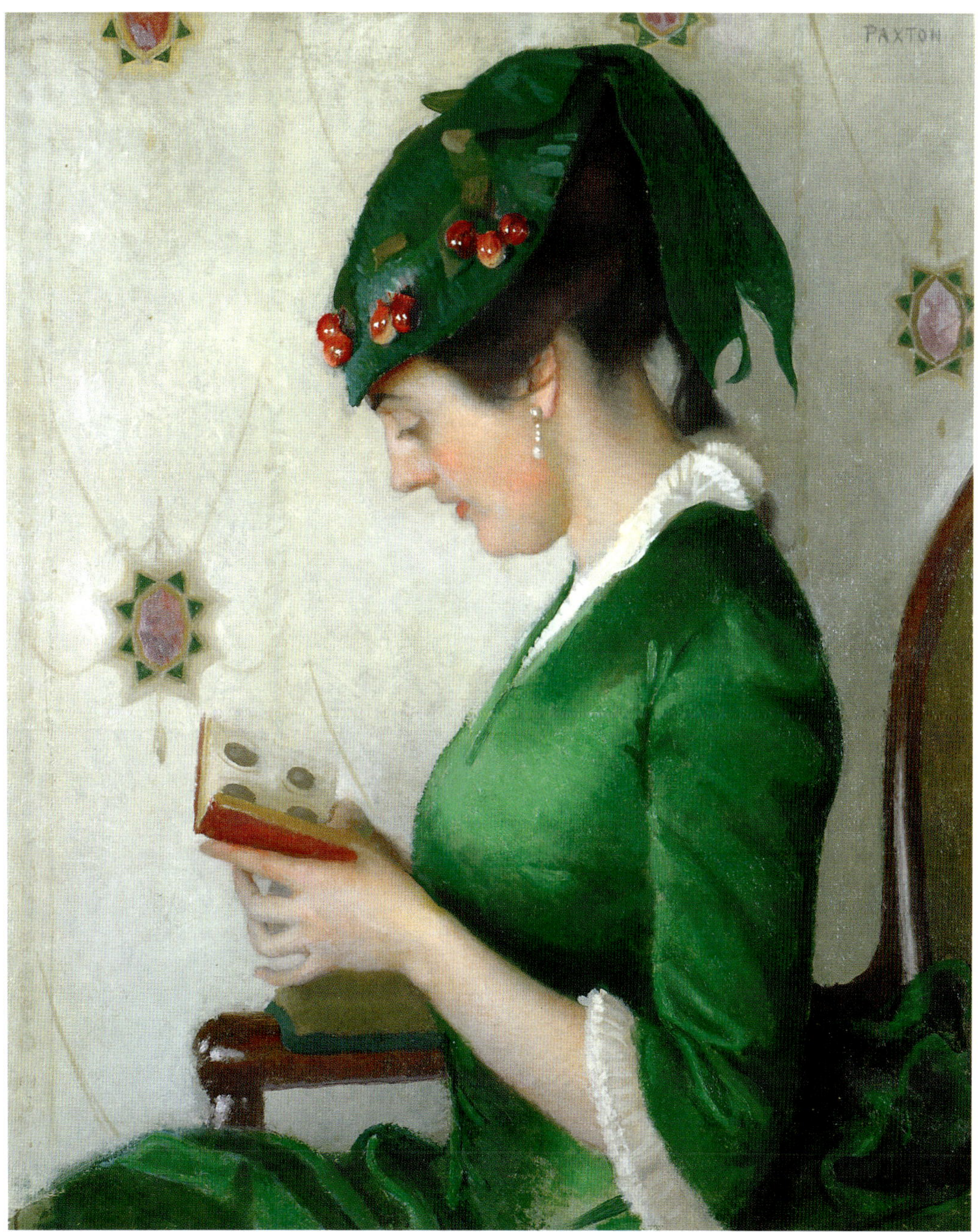


**No. 34**

William Paxton (American, 1869-1941)
*The Album*, ca. 1913
Oil on canvas
30 x 25 inches
Collection of Barbara Guillaume Griffin

# *James Peale*

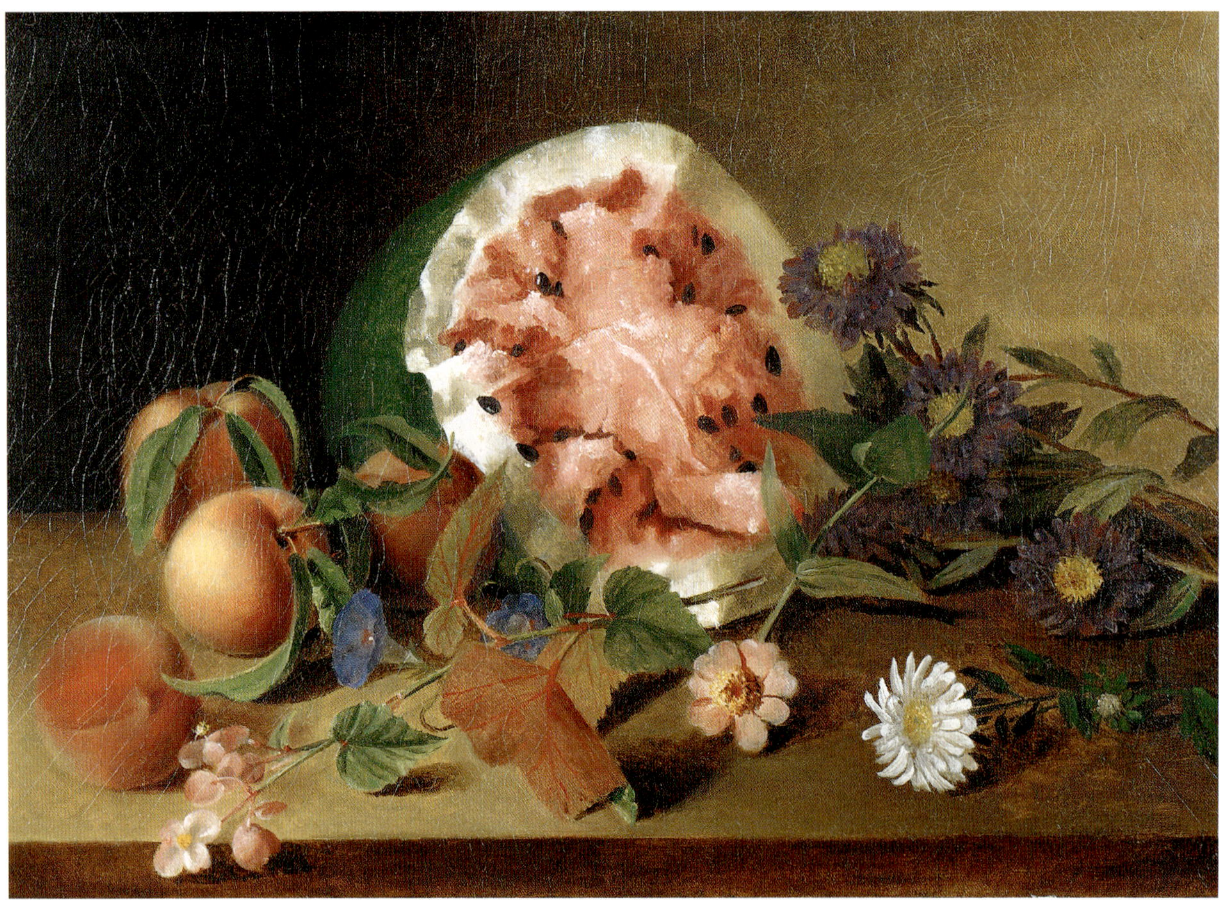

**No. 35**

James Peale (American, 1749-1831)
*Still-Life with Watermelon*, ca. 1829
Oil on canvas
16 x 22 inches
Collection of Mr. and Mrs. Noel Wadsworth

REFERRED TO AS THE CITY of Enlightenment, Philadelphia was home to the celebrated Peale family of artists, including James, his brother Charles Willson, his nephews Raphaelle and Rembrandt, and his daughters Sarah Miriam and Anna Claypoole. James, always seeking steady patronage, did not limit himself to the genre of still-life. He worked in the varied fields of portraiture, miniature, and landscape throughout his long career and exhibited regularly at all the major artistic centers of nineteenth-century America.[1] The widespread exhibition of works by the Peale family established their place within emerging American art and helped to create a tradition that would last well into the late nineteenth century. Still-lifes were first intended as a form of scientific documentation; artists studied the field of botany through floral still-lifes. Later, it was celebrated as a form of deceptive illusion by Raphaelle Peale. James was the most painterly of the group, caring less for trompe-l'oeil compositions and more for the varied textures and coloristic subtleties of the objects. While the artists differed in technique, their compositional arrangements reveal their obvious exchanges and their mutual reliance upon seventeenth-century Dutch precedents. Nearly all still-life painters of the late eighteenth and early nineteenth centuries created simple tabletops upon which a balanced arrangement of fruit and flowers is diagonally lit. Artists emphasized the classical qualities of control and symmetry in their compositions, in accordance with the popular Federal style. Academic circles promoted the same characteristics in portraiture, landscape painting, and architectural design.

*Still-Life with Watermelon*, executed two years before the artist's death, presents a fruit and flower arrangement within a relatively shallow space in front of a diagonally lit background. Peale employed his favorite prop of the broken watermelon as the apex of the composition. He consciously juxtaposed the succulent interior of the melon with the smooth, round peaches to accentuate the texture of the fleshy fruit. While the fruit appears ripe, the leaves lying limply over the farthest peach indicate a concern with the passage of time. Peale often adapted the Dutch theme of *vanitas* within his still-lifes with images of bruised fruit or flowers with wilted petals and leaves. The orderly, balanced, and frontal presentation of the table top places *Still-Life with Watermelon* firmly in the tradition of Classicism without the overt trappings of columns, pediments, or classical themes. The simplicity of the image signifies the early American penchant for order in a disorderly world as a demonstration of the success of American society in imposing its will over unruly nature.

---

1 Biographical material taken from Wolfgang Born, *Still-Life Painting in America* (New York: Oxford University Press, 1947); Nicolai Cikovsky, *Raphaelle Peale Still-Lifes*, Exhib. cat. (New York: Harry N. Abrams, Inc., 1988); and William H. Gerdts and Russell Burke, *American Still-Life Painting* (New York: Praeger Publishers, 1971).

# *Lilla Cabot Perry*

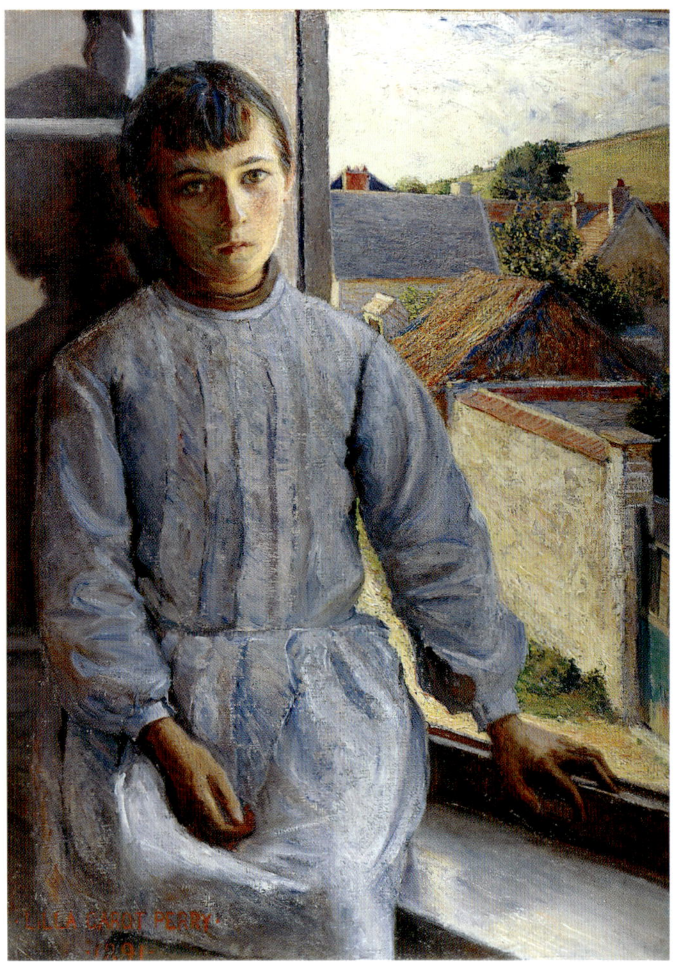

~ **No. 36** ~

LILLA CABOT PERRY (AMERICAN, 1848-1933)
*Angela*, 1891
Oil on canvas
36 ¼ x 27 inches
Collection of Mr. and Mrs. Jack Huber

UNTIL FAIRLY RECENTLY, Lilla Cabot Perry's reputation has rested on her close relationship with Claude Monet and her efforts to promote Impressionism in America. A re-examination of her oeuvre, however, reveals her singular talent and remarkable rise to the top of Boston's art scene. Unlike her female contemporaries, who were forced to choose between career and family, Perry enjoyed both, taking up painting professionally only after marriage and the birth of her three children. She began her art training at the Cowles School in Boston under Dennis Bunker and Robert Vonnoh and continued her education in Paris at the Académie Colarossi and the Académie Julian. Perry worked alongside male colleagues in France, Germany, Italy, and Spain, and was the only American woman artist of her time to live and work in Japan. In 1889, the Georges Petit Gallery hosted a large exhibition of paintings by Claude Monet, which altered Perry's future as an artist. She later remembered the work as exhibiting a "clearness of vision and a fidelity to nature such as I had never seen before." [1] Monet's work sparked the Perry family's first summer in Giverny, which quickly became a favorite retreat. She joined the small artists' colony headed by Theodore Robinson, John Breck, and Theodore Butler, who had similarly discovered the power of Monet's *plein-air* masterpieces and the charms of the village downstream from Paris. Perry returned home to promote Impressionism within the elite circles of Boston society. By exhibiting works by Monet and Breck in her home, Perry was responsible, in part, for the movement's acceptance in Boston. Her own paintings were regularly exhibited in the exclusive salons of Europe and America and garnered praise from critics, one of whom proclaimed, "Lilla Cabot Perry's brush practically wrote the history of contemporary art development in America from its earliest indebtedness to the French and German academies to its own flowering." [2]

Perry's three children often appear in her paintings and constitute a major theme of her work. *Alice in a White Hat* depicts her youngest child, Alice Perry Grew, whose striking beauty made her an ideal model. Perry goes beyond mere beauty, however, to suggest a melancholy behind the downcast eyes of her daughter. The reserved nature of the sitter contrasts with the quickly wrought forms and spontaneity of pastel.

The influence of her colleagues in Giverny resulted in an immediate change in Perry's style. She abandoned the academic technique found in her earlier portraits in favor of a bright palette applied with broken brushstrokes. Completed during the Perrys' second summer in Giverny, *Angela*, a portrait of a young French peasant girl, exhibits Perry's new concern for light and color. While the palette is bright, the overall atmosphere of the work is one of alienation and withdrawal. The window, which frames a beautiful Norman landscape, also confines the young girl indoors. Many of Perry's Impressionist pictures are brighter; however, Impressionism was not a one-dimensional experience for her. Many of the new Symbolist painters, working nearby in Pont-Aven, were experimenting with a style more like what is found in this picture.

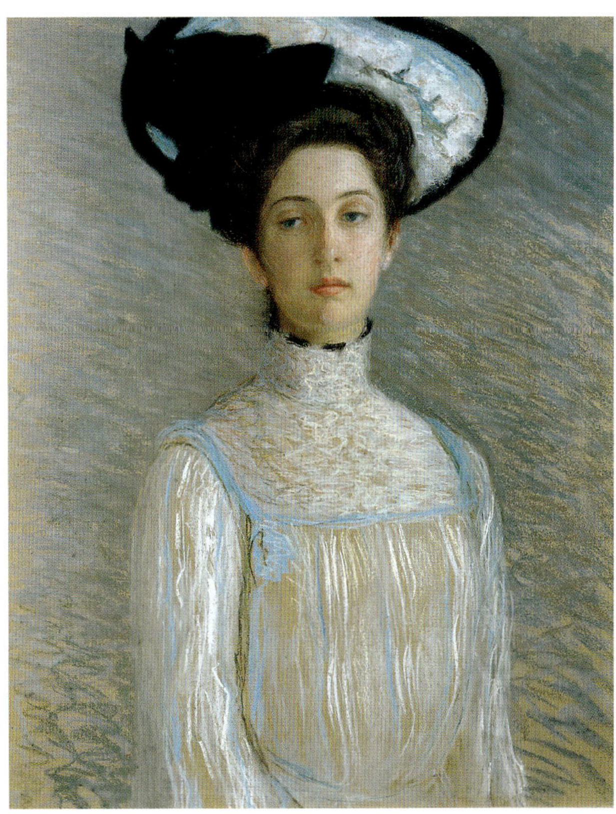

**No. 37**

LILLA CABOT PERRY (AMERICAN, 1848-1933)
*Alice in a White Hat*, 1904
Pastel on paper mounted on canvas
31 ½ x 25 ½ inches
Collection of Dr. and Mrs. Jeb Stewart

1 Lilla Cabot Perry, "Reminiscences of Claude Monet From 1889-1909," *American Magazine of Art* 18 (March 1927): 119, quoted in Gerdts, *Masterworks of American Impressionism from the Pfeil Collection*, 195.

2 Albert Franz Cochrane, *Boston Evening Transcript*, 28 October 1933, *Memorial Exhibition of Paintings by Lilla Cabot Perry*, Boston Art Club, quoted in Meredith Martindale, *Lilla Cabot Perry: An American Impressionist* (Washington, D.C.: The National Museum of Women in the Arts, 1990), 15.

# *William Trost Richards*

William Trost Richards's early love for nature was visible not in his paintings but rather in his prose. A member of the "Forensic and Literary Circle" of Philadelphia during high school, Richards wrote numerous romantic essays that focused on the riotous beauty of America's landscapes. Later, these words would take visual form in his art. He began his career as an ornamental copyist for the firm Archer, Warner and Miskey. He created meticulously detailed designs for them and studied fine art with the German portrait and landscape painter Paul Weber. His developing commitment to landscape art was strengthened after a sketching trip to the Catskill Mountains. In the Romantic spirit of his predecessors Thomas Cole and Frederic Edwin Church, Richards spoke of his "desire that will not rest satisfied 'till landscape can tell stories to the human heart and be a medium of noble and powerful expression even as the human countenance."[1] Richards portrayed nature with a scrupulous fidelity to detail characteristic of the Düsseldorf style, which he had seen during his travels abroad. Similarly, the writings of Sir John Ruskin and the paintings of the American Pre-Raphaelites emphasized the importance of "the minute & faithful representation of details." In 1866, Richards returned to Europe, where he worked in Paris, Venice, Florence, Rome, and Naples. Upon his return to America late in 1867, he turned increasingly to American coastal subjects and traveled along the eastern shore to make sketches of varying "combinations of rock and beach and sea" that he later converted to finished works at his studio in Germantown, on the outskirts of Philadelphia.[2] In 1878, Richards traveled to England, where he remained for two years. When he returned to America in 1880, he found patrons had grown tired of the Pre-Raphaelite fascination with realism and had become increasingly intrigued with the looser and more subjective Tonalism and Impressionism practiced by many young American painters. Nonetheless, the last quarter of Richards's life was full and busy, with frequent trips to Europe. In 1905, the year of his death, Richards was honored by the Pennsylvania Academy with a Gold Medal of Honor.

Richards, a member of the American Society of Water Colors, increasingly utilized the medium for his marine subject matter. The spontaneity associated with the looser medium is generally absent from his detailed seascapes. In his later works, one senses a greater subtlety in his application of paint, where reality is softened somewhat by a luminosity foreign to his Pre-Raphaelite beginnings. *Cliffs Overlooking Bay* is one of a series of large watercolors illustrating

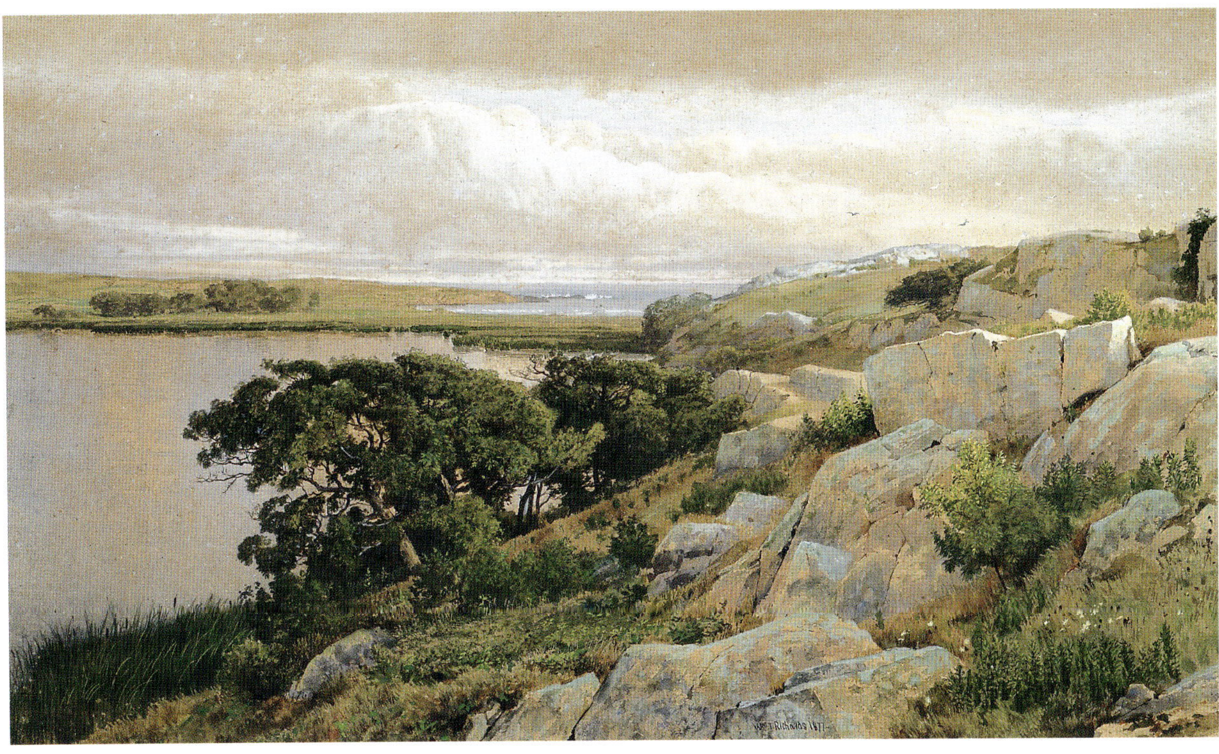

~ **No. 38** ~

William Trost Richards (American, 1833-1905)
*Cliffs Overlooking Bay*, 1877
Watercolor and gouache on paper
22 15/16 x 36 3/4 inches
High Museum of Art, Atlanta
Purchase with funds from the Members Guild in honor of the 10th anniversary of Gudmund Vigtel as Director of the High Museum of Art, 73.54

well-known locations on the southern side of the Newport Peninsula. The critical and commercial success of the series was immediate. *Appleton's Art Journal* stated, "W.T. Richards appears this year in a new style, much more upon the idea of a true gradation of light and shade than in the delicate sea-pictures, or in the landscapes which have hitherto come from his hand."[3]

---

1 William Trost Richards, quoted in Linda S. Ferber, *William Trost Richards: American Landscape and Marine Painter (1833-1905)*, Exhib. cat. (Brooklyn: The Brooklyn Museum of Art, 1973), 15.

2 Ibid., 31.

3 Ibid., 32.

# Severin Roesen

The German-born still-life artist Severin Roesen arrived in America in 1848; after a brief stay in New York, he settled in the affluent lumber community of Williamsport, Pennsylvania. Williamsport was home to a new generation of businessmen who had quickly taken advantage of central Pennsylvania's rich natural resources; as business in the region prospered, artists and craftsmen found themselves in high demand. Roesen, benefiting from this trend, completed over two hundred paintings during his twelve-year stay there.[1] The abundant and ornate presentation of flowers and fruits that adorn Roesen's compositions appear almost gaudy compared to the simple arrangements of his predecessor James Peale; however, Roesen was working within a very different climate of middle-class prosperity,[2] and he consistently used the plainer tableware and baskets that could be found in a typical middle-class home.

The reasons that Roesen left Williamsport and returned to New York in 1872 are not clear. Some scholars believe Roesen returned to broaden his market, while others believe that his motivation was to attend his eldest daughter's wedding. Regardless, his last extant painting was composed during his final year in Williamsport.

Roesen tended to work from a distinct repertoire of objects, repeating standard motifs in slightly varied arrangements. Roesen's remarkable draftsmanship made his still-life elements come alive and inspired the trompe-l'oeil work of William Harnett and Richard Goodwin. *Fruit Still-Life with Wine Glass* exists in at least ten other versions, of which only two are signed.[3] Roesen has, in each painting, arranged a cornucopia of fruit spilling from a two-tiered table. He took pleasure in describing the varying textures of the fruits, going so far as to peel a lemon and quarter an orange to demonstrate his ability to depict flesh as well as rind. The elaborate tendrils of the grape clusters are a hallmark of Roesen's still-lifes and function in his signed works as the script (see detail, pp. 66-67).

---

1 Biographical information taken from William H. Gerdts, *Painters of the Humble Truth: Masterpieces of American Still-Life, 1801-1939* (Columbia: The University of Missouri Press, 1981); Judith Hansen O'Toole, *Severin Roesen* (Lewisburg, Pennsylvania: Bucknell University Press, 1992); and John Wilmerding, *An American Perspective: Nineteenth-Century Art from the Collection of JoAnn & Julian Ganz, Jr.* (Washington, D.C.: National Gallery of Art, 1981).

2 Wilmerding, 91.

3 Judith O'Toole makes this observation but must have been unaware of the Roesen in the Coopers' collection, which follows the same formula as her illustrated example. As Roesen often used these works to barter for town services it is not unusual that many versions exist. In addition, as O'Toole notes, Roesen was working at a time when popular prints were entering the market place as affordable, quality works of art. Artists often responded by turning out several versions of a popular composition, 33.

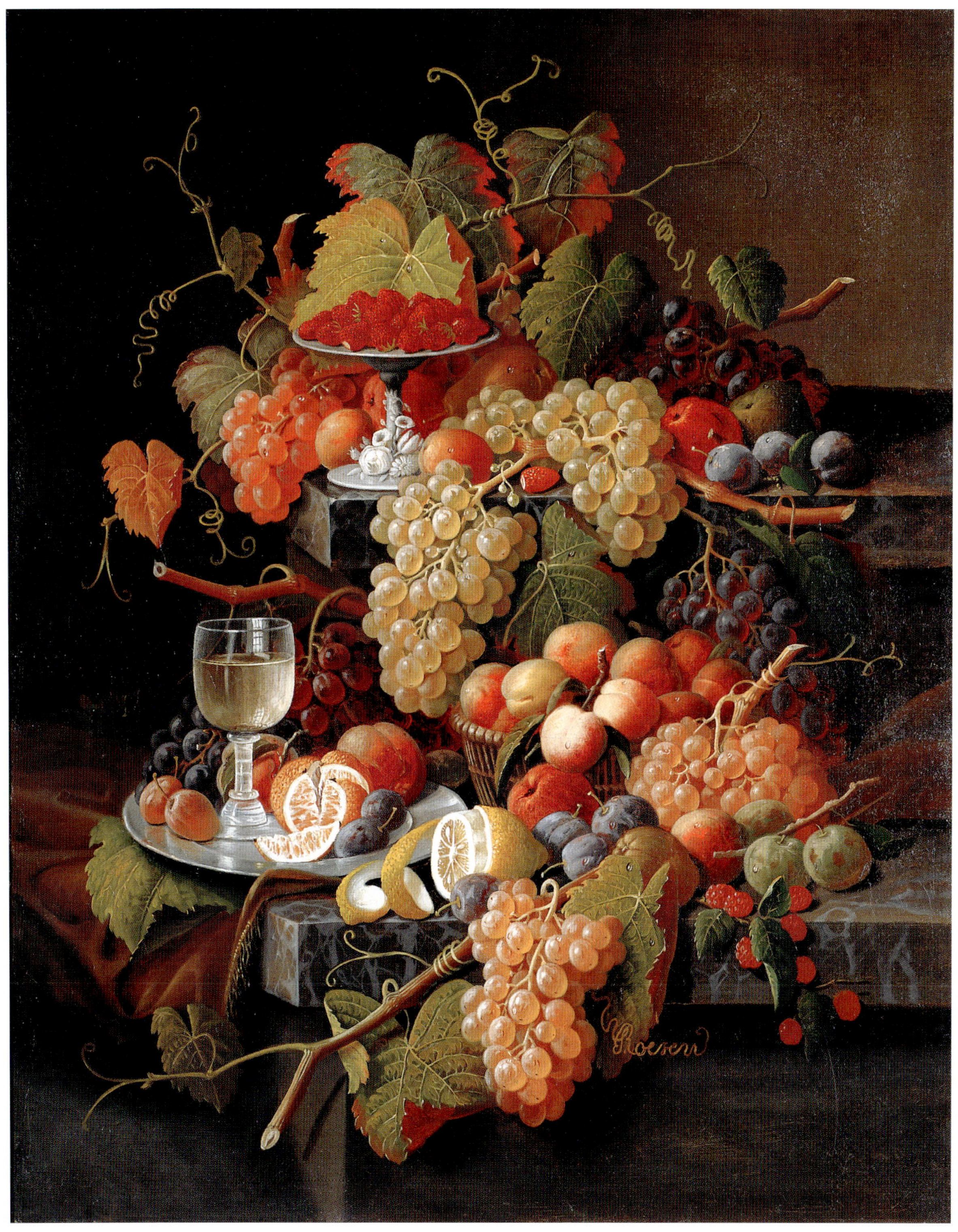

**No. 39**

SEVERIN ROESEN (GERMAN, ACTIVE 1847-72), *Fruit Still-Life with Wine Glass.*
Oil on canvas, 35 ½ x 28 ½ inches. Collection of Dr. and Mrs. Tom Cooper.

# John Singer Sargent

THE COSMOPOLITAN PAINTER John Singer Sargent was described in 1924 by critic William Starkweather as "an American, born in Italy, educated in France, who looks like a German, speaks like an Englishman, and paints like a Spaniard." This oft-quoted observation demonstrates Sargent's established reputation as a sophisticated European and the international acclaim of his artistic achievement, particularly remarkable because American countrymen of his youth were notably nativist in their cultural beliefs. Sargent, born in Florence to American expatriates, spent his youth studying intermittently at the Accademia di Belle Arti. He entered the independent atelier of Parisian portrait painter Emile Carolus-Duran in 1874 and quickly adopted his mentor's painterly technique. Carolus-Duran, unlike the traditional French academics, emphasized surface texture, color, and light. Sargent's success under Carolus-Duran resulted in his acceptance into numerous Parisian salons in 1877 and his inclusion of *The Oyster Gatherers of Cancale* (Boston Museum of Fine Arts) in the first exhibition of the Society of American Artists in New York in 1878. These years were punctuated by periodic trips to Capri, Tangier, Morocco, and Venice, where Sargent, stimulated by the examples of Renaissance paintings by Titian and his followers, focused increasingly on the process of painting. His exposure to the work of Diego Velázquez and Frans Hals in Spain and to seventeenth-century Dutch paintings further restricted his tonal range, deepened his palette, and provided a model for the simplicity of Sargent's compositions. This art-for-art's-sake approach to painting irrevocably attached Sargent to the developing modernist movement. The exhibition of his portrait of Madame Pierre Gautreau, *Madame X* (Metropolitan Museum of Art), at the Salon of 1884 brought him instant notoriety. The highly sensualized depiction of the married aristocrat introduced the femme-fatale to polite Parisian society. When he was not working in the grand portrait manner, Sargent incorporated the Impressionist aesthetic of his friend Claude Monet into his landscape studies. Portraiture, however, remained his passion. In 1887, he moved to Massachusetts, where his reputation as a society portraitist who edited reality garnered him immediate commissions. Over the next four years, Sargent painted nearly sixty portraits for members of New England's upper class, while still maintaining an active exhibition schedule abroad. Sargent was elected an academician of both London's Royal Academy and New York's National Academy of Design in 1897. He gave up portrait commissions in 1908, but continued to execute informal charcoal drawings of friends and family. Sargent's late efforts reflect the same candor, naturalism, psychological nuance, and florid brushwork that characterize his entire oeuvre.[1]

Sargent's flattering brush was not limited to aristocratic women in their prime. He executed numerous refined portraits of men and children that in their elegance defy the nature of their very being. His delicate portrait of Jeanne Kieffer demonstrates the same studied casualness and calculated aesthetic concerns of Sargent's later works. A tour-de-force of painting, the portrait presents the young aristocrat adorned with a cross. Her pink dress edged with white lace and her jeweled necklace speak not only of her advertised faith but also of her family's wealth. She looks directly at the viewer, not in a confrontational way, but with a maturity beyond her years. Sargent's subtle palette and simple composition showcase his bravura brushwork and refined drawing. Painted when Sargent was still establishing his reputation, this portrait clearly indicates his future success.

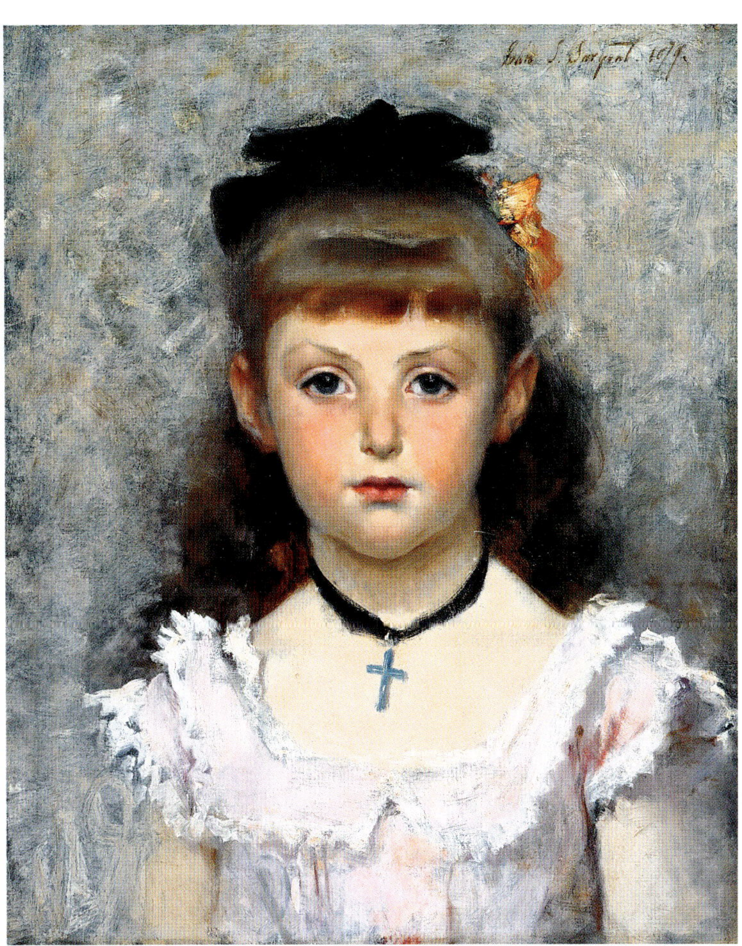

**No. 40**

JOHN SINGER SARGENT (AMERICAN, 1856-1925)
*Portrait of Jeanne Kieffer*, 1879
Oil on canvas
18 x 15 inches
Collection of Mrs. Deen Day Smith

---

1 Biographical information taken from Trevor J. Fairbrother, *John Singer Sargent* (New York: Harry N. Abrams in association with the National Museum of American Art, 1994); Patricia Hills, *John Singer Sargent*, Exhib. cat. (New York: Whitney Museum of American Art and Harry N. Abrams, 1986); and Marc Simpson, *Uncanny Spectacle: The Public Career of the Young John Singer Sargent*, Exhib. cat. (New Haven: Yale University Press, 1997).

# Henry Schnakenberg

Born in New Brighton, New York, Henry Schnakenberg began his career working in the insurance business. In 1913, he joined three hundred thousand other Americans to view the potent display of European modernism at the Armory Show. Inspired, Schnakenberg decided to pursue art full-time and enrolled at the Art Students League. Like those of fellow students Reginald Marsh and Isabel Bishop, Schnakenberg's crowded compositions reflect the influence of his teachers, Kenneth Hayes Miller and John Sloan. Visually frenetic in organization and spirit, their work expressed the rhythm of popular culture, which by the 1930s had changed into a culture of sight and sound. Neon street signs, subways, buxom shoppers, hurried businessmen, and working-class immigrants crowded into compositions and became part of what one critic referred to as the "crowd movement à la mode."[1] Depictions of the urban scene, popularized by Sloan and promoted by the Social Realists, fascinated Schnakenberg, who filtered contemporary fact through his own consciousness. He was a populist painter who viewed his subjects with a mixture of disdain and compassion. Encouraged by successful exhibitions, Schnakenberg began teaching at the Art Students League in 1923 and later succeeded Sloan as president of the League in 1932.

Schnakenberg's portrayal of a subway terminal on West 79th Street demonstrates his dark, satirical view of urban life. City dwellers are represented by caricatured types: the drab immigrant flower salesman, the middle-class brassy blonde shopper, the generalized, faceless businessman dressed in trenchcoat and hat, and the wide-eyed child surrounded by questionable characters all inhabit *West Side*. Schnakenberg expressed the alienation and disconnectedness that were symptoms of the new-found moral freedoms and energized society of the modern metropolis. The pedestrians appear, as implied by the wording on the frosted subway station window, as if in a trance, psychologically cut off from their fellow man. The dark palette and stormy sky contribute to the overall unease of the Depression-era setting. Working alongside Reginald Marsh and Social Realists, Schnakenberg presented a glimpse of both the positive and negative sides of urban life.

---

1 *The American Magazine of Art* 28 (January 1935): 62.

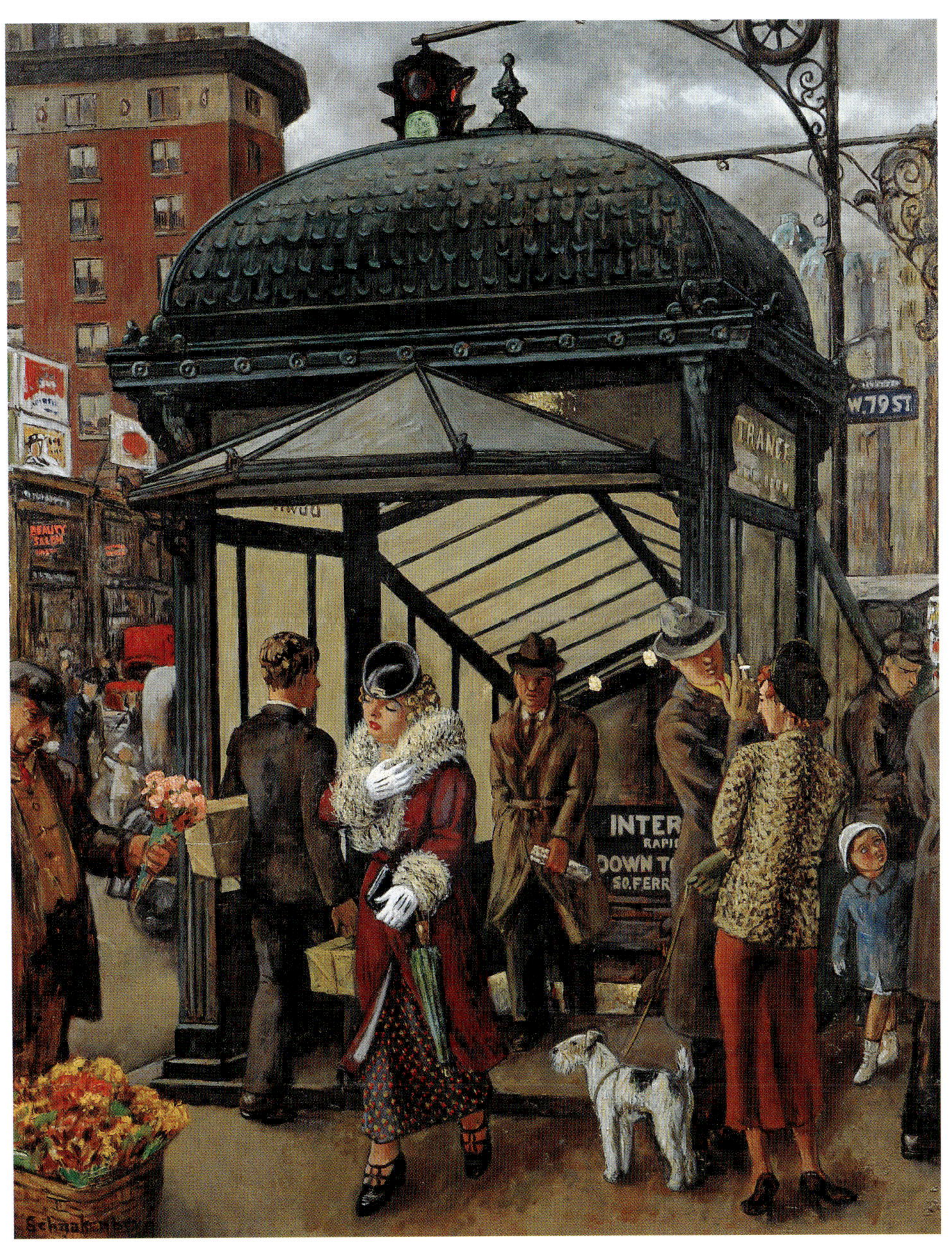


**No. 41**

HENRY SCHNAKENBERG (AMERICAN, 1892-1970)
*West Side*, 1935
Oil on canvas
45 x 36 inches
Collection of the Columbus Museum, Columbus, Georgia.
Museum purchase made possible by Norman S. Rothschild
in honor of his parents, Aleen and Irwin B. Rothschild.

# Joseph Henry Sharp

Joseph Henry Sharp was only sixteen years old when General George Custer and his cavalry were massacred at the Battle of Little Bighorn, but the widely publicized account struck the young artist deeply. Raised in Bridgeport, Ohio, Sharp spent his early childhood reading and dreaming about the exotic "noble red man" detailed in James Fenimore Cooper's romanticized *Leather-stocking Tales.* After a nearly fatal childhood accident, he was left deaf and turned increasingly to the visual arts as a means of communication. His interest in art was encouraged by his parents, who sent the fourteen-year-old to Cincinnati to study at the McMicken School of Design, where he befriended fellow artists Frank Duveneck, Robert Blume, Edward Potthast, and Henry Farny. After three years at the school, Sharp joined the growing number of American artists in Europe seeking further education. He studied for a year with renowned portrait painter Charles Verlat at the Antwerp Academy of Fine Arts and took brief excursions to the Netherlands, France, and Germany. He returned to America in 1882 and established a studio near Farny in Cincinnati, where the two discussed the myths and mysteries surrounding America's fabled indigenous cultures. Stirred by the ever-present Western dime-store novel and the even more exciting newspaper accounts of Billy the Kid, the Earp brothers, and Doc Holliday, Sharp headed west in 1883 on the first of many trips.

After his first journey west, Sharp's commitment to his craft led him once again to Europe to study at the Académie Julian, where he remained until 1889. Upon his return to Cincinnati, Sharp, frustrated with the mundane but profitable art of commissioned portraiture, began plans for another trip west. In 1893, he met his friend, fellow artist John Hauser, in Santa Fe; the two traveled throughout the Northern Plains sketching the Pueblo Indians. Sharp worked as an art instructor at the Cincinnati Art Academy from 1892 until 1903, but spent the summers painting portraits of men, women, and children in the settlement of Taos, New Mexico. Each of Sharp's celebrated paintings from these years imbues his sitters with the dignity that the United States government was actively stripping away. Although life in the pueblos was relatively stable, the Plains Indians were rapidly becoming Anglicized. Sharp journeyed north to document the disappearing tribal culture of the Crow, Sioux, Blackfoot, and Cheyenne tribes in Montana, Wyoming, and the Dakotas and eventually settled at the Crow Agency in Montana. Museums and galleries praised Sharp's work not only for its sympathetic and moving depictions of

Indian life but also for the artist's invaluable ethnological contributions. This truth, however, often existed alongside the romanticized and sentimentalized depictions of what in reality was an extremely difficult existence plagued by disease, alcoholism, and poverty.

Along with Bert Phillips, Ernest Blumenschein, Oscar Berninghaus, Herbert Dunton, and Irving Couse, Sharp was a founding member of the Taos Society of Artists, a self-promoting group that organized traveling exhibitions of members' work. Sharp traveled continually throughout the rest of his career, spending time in Hawaii, Asia, and Mexico, yet he always returned to the West for inspiration.[1]

During Sharp's prolific career, he created over 10,500 paintings, watercolors, monotypes, pastels, and etchings, over two-thirds of which portrayed Native Americans. *Indian Encampment* is one of many idealized Crow camp scenes that Sharp painted in Montana. The artist spent the fall and winter months at the Crow Agency making the "snowy landscape, sage brush foothills, and winter foliage along the Little Bighorn River . . . more paintable." His studio window looked out over fields that, during council meetings and the annual Crow Fair, were heavily populated by many Plains tribes. While Sharp alluded to the industrialization of tribal life with the leather saddles and rifles, he carefully excluded the presence of the white men who lived side by side with the natives at the Crow Agency. Sharp was one of the true witnesses to the changing character of Native Americans, yet his paintings revealed little of their difficult existence.

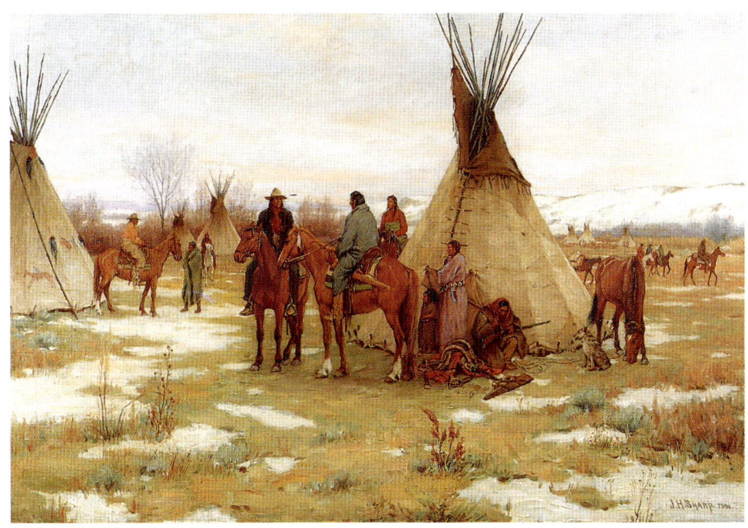

**No. 42**

JOSEPH HENRY SHARP (AMERICAN, 1859-1953)
*Indian Encampment*, 1906
Oil on canvas
26 ½ x 39 ¾ inches
Albany Museum of Art; gift of Henry M. Goodyear, M.D., at the request of his son, Mr. Henry M. Goodyear, Jr.

1 Biographical material taken from Forest Fenn, *The Beat of the Drum and the Whoop of the Dance: The Study of the Life and Work of Joseph Henry Sharp* (Santa Fe: Fenn Publishing Company, 1983).

# *John Sloan*

JOHN SLOAN WAS BORN IN LOCK Haven, a small community in scenic central Pennsylvania. At age twenty-two, he enrolled at the Pennsylvania Academy of the Fine Arts and supported himself by working in the art department of the *Philadelphia Inquirer.* It was around this time that his long association with Robert Henri began. As Sloan remembered, Henri "had a studio at 806 Walnut Street where we used to gather once a week to talk and listen to his ideas about painting, and about what it meant to be an artist. . . ." Henri's vision became Sloan's, and the two artists, along with William Glackens, George Luks, and Everett Shinn, produced a body of work that celebrated their urban surroundings. In 1903, Sloan joined his colleagues in New York and began documenting lower-class and working-class people. His compositions, which often portrayed prostitutes and bums, did not escape criticism, as evidenced by the American Water Color Society's decision not to exhibit four of Sloan's etchings from his series on life in New York due to their "vulgar" content. While deemed unfit in academic circles, these realistic scenes revealed his immense artistic energy, his sympathetic love of humanity, and the depth of his artistic insight. Sloan's exposure to the work of Georges Braque, Pablo Picasso, Vincent van Gogh, and Paul Cézanne at the Armory Show, coupled with his ongoing experiments with Hardesty Maratta's theories of color and design, prompted him to refocus on the "sign-making graphics of painting."[1] His new motivation to create was evident in a letter to his friend John Quinn: "The 'new movements in Art' add a lot to one's enthusiasm in work, have a rather electrifying effect on the general atmosphere, broaden one's horizon, smash molds and declare liberty."[2] His independent spirit took form in politics as well as art. An active member of the Communist party and editor of *The Masses* until 1916, Sloan shared his radical political views with both his pupils at the Art Students League and his colleagues in the Society of Independent Artists. Throughout his long career, Sloan remained a modernist in every sense of the word and continued to experiment with technique and subject matter.[3]

While Sloan is primarily known for his depictions of urban life, his *plein-air* seascapes and landscapes of Gloucester, Massachusetts, demonstrate his ability to infuse humanity and nature with a poetic spirit. Sloan spent five productive summers in the seaside community, which he described as "one of the odd corners of America, built against the Puritan landscape, blue-eyed and rocky."[4] Inspired to return to pure painting, Sloan created works like *Tittering Girls* to celebrate texture, form, and color devoid of political or social implications. During these years, Sloan was separating himself from *The Masses* and turning to the purely formal, painterly problems found in landscape painting. Sloan

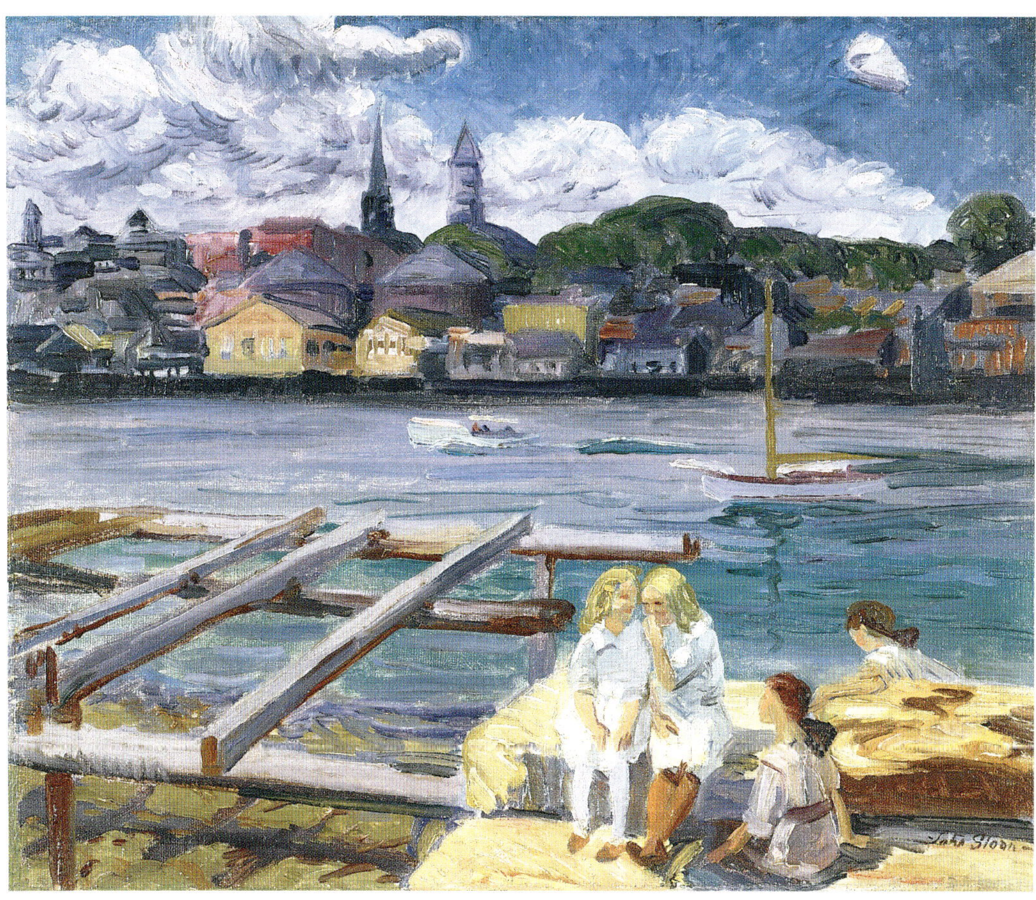


**No. 43**

JOHN SLOAN (AMERICAN, 1871-1951)
*Tittering Girls*, 1915
Oil on canvas
20 x 24 inches
Collection of Mr. and Mrs. Jack Huber

was interested not in replicating nature but rather in capturing the vital essence of the coastal landscape through a limited palette and selective vision. In *Tittering Girls*, he presents the bright harbor of Gloucester, defined by the same color combination as the church steeples in the background. Gloucester had also attracted the attention of several Impressionists, including Childe Hassam and Willard Metcalf. It is a testament to the often parallel aesthetics of the two apparently warring camps in American art at the turn of the century–the realists and the Impressionists–that they often come so close together. Sloan's painting expresses much the same celebration as the Impressionists' of brilliant sunlight and exhilarating nature.

---

1 John Sloan Notes, quoted in Grant Holcolmbe, *John Sloan: The Gloucester Years,* Exhib. cat. (Springfield: Springfield Museum and Library, 1980), 10.

2 Quoted in ibid., 11.

3 Biographical material taken from ibid.; *John Sloan: Paintings, Prints and Drawings*, Exhib. cat. (Hanover, New Hampshire: Dartmouth College, 1981); and Patterson Sims, *John Sloan: A Concentration of Works from the Permanent Collection of the Whitney Museum of Art* (New York: Whitney Museum of American Art, 1980).

4 *New York Times*, 22 February 1925, quoted in Sims, 12.

# Attributed to John Smibert

JOHN SMIBERT BEGAN HIS CAREER as an apprentice to a house painter and plasterer in his hometown of Edinburgh, Scotland. At age twenty-one, he moved to London, which was then a center of artistic activity due to England's rapid economic growth and its society's increasing sophistication and desire to own art. Smibert worked as an ornamental coach painter but sharpened his technical skills as a copyist for galleries. Although this type of art was considered the lowest form of painting, Smibert used the opportunity to become familiar with various collectors and art dealers while improving his technique. After a brief enrollment at the Great Queen Street Academy and a short trial as a portrait painter in Edinburgh, Smibert went to Italy in 1719 and spent the next three years studying in Florence, Rome, and Naples. In addition to the prestige afforded artists with Continental experience, the prospect of patronage from tourists was an enticing reason to travel to Italy. Many British visitors commissioned copies of Old Master paintings as well as portraits of themselves, while others required assistance with their growing collections; Smibert performed both duties while abroad. He returned to London in the summer of 1722 and set up a studio in the popular art community near Covent Garden on the Strand. Here, he painted "elevated portraits," in which he sought to imbue sitters with nobility and virtue regardless of their stations in

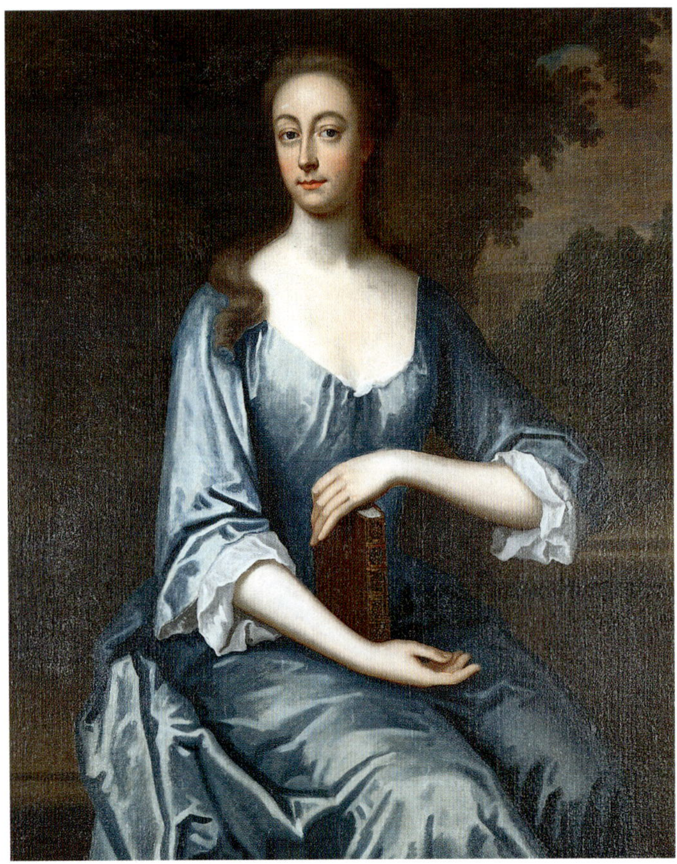

**No. 44**

ATTRIBUTED TO JOHN SMIBERT
(ENGLISH, 1688-1751)
*Lady in Blue*, 1735
Oil on canvas
44 x 36 inches
Collection of Mr. and Mrs. Henry D. Green

life. Characterized by a language of rationalism and rules, Smibert's compositions adhered to the Platonic philosophy of reason's precedence over emotion. Although Smibert was a popular portraitist in London, he decided to join his friend Reverend George Berkeley, who planned to establish a college in Bermuda. Smibert was to be a professor of art as part of Berkeley's newly formed liberal studies program. After numerous problems were revealed in Berkeley's plan, however, the college was relocated to the pluralistic community of Rhode Island. En route, Smibert stopped for what was intended to be a three-day visit in Boston; he later became a permanent resident. In Boston, he continued the British portrait tradition and his painting rooms, with casts and copies after the Old Masters, became the closest thing to a formal painting school in the city. His depictions of Americans show little departure from his earlier formulaic approach. His other business endeavors, including the opening of Boston's first comprehensive "colour shop" and the sale of European prints, supplemented his waning income in portraiture. In these years, Smibert became increasingly interested in landscape painting, architecture, and informal teaching.[1]

*Lady in Blue*, attributed to Smibert and probably a portrait of Lady Sunderland, is typical of the artist's standardized depictions of women. Although patrons desired a certain resemblance, women in particular preferred an overall sense of beauty to dominate their portraits. Ever conscious of maintaining a thriving business, Smibert never failed to sacrifice a sitter's individual characteristics in favor of a flattering por trait. Indeed, while the present subject appears in her youthful prime, she could have been anywhere from sixteen to sixty years old. Smibert represents her financial prosperity with a backdrop of cultivated land and refers to her role as a civilizing influence with the delicately embraced book. Indeed, prior to the establishment of public schools, colonial women were expected to nurture the cultural development of their families. Since the vast majority of Smibert's sitters appear in a similar blue dress, the choice of clothing speaks less to the fashion of the day than it does to artistic convention. Women were to be painted so that "they appear generally at home in a loose deshabille which, in a manner, half hides and half displays their charms." [2] Smibert's portrait represents the sitter as a model of colonial perfection.

---

1 Biographical information taken from Richard H. Saunders, *John Smibert: Colonial America's First Portrait Painter* (New Haven: Yale University Press, 1995).

2 Quoted from a contemporary source, Historical Society of Pennsylvania, Philadelphia (Bridenbaugh, 1948), 136, cited in ibid., 77.

# Lilly Martin Spencer

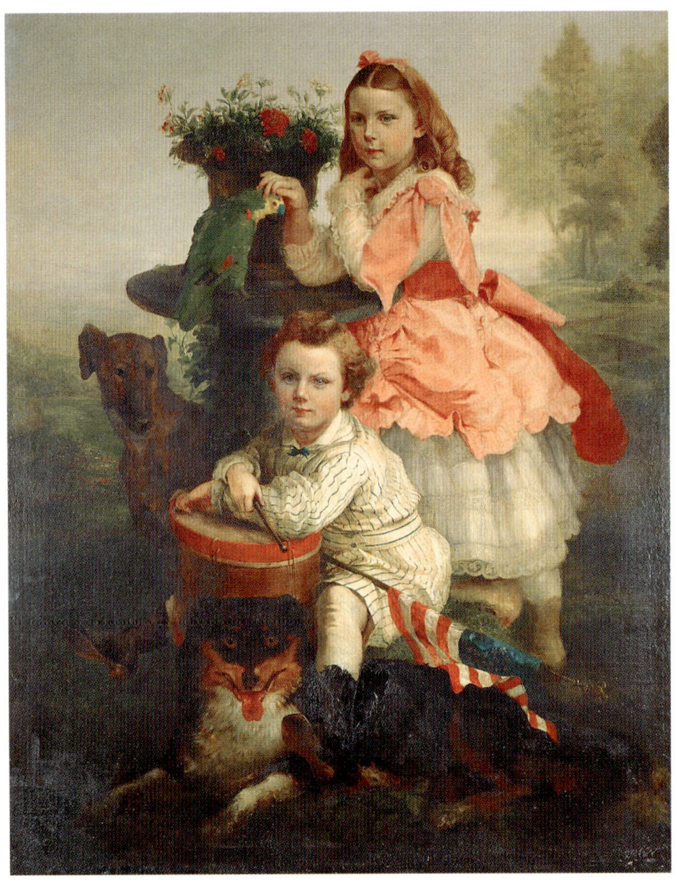

~ No. 45 ~

LILLY MARTIN SPENCER (AMERICAN, 1822-1902)
*Our Future Americans*, ca. 1865
Oil on canvas
62 x 51 inches
Collection of Mr. and Mrs. Otis T. Brumby

LILLY MARTIN SPENCER, the daughter of French immigrants, arrived in America in 1830. The Martins settled in Marietta, Ohio, where they were active in the temperance, abolitionist, and women's suffrage movements. Spencer was home-schooled at the family farm at Devol's Dam. Her father was a lecturer at the Collegiate Institute and Western Teaching Seminary. Her budding artistic talent was recognized by two local artists, Sala Bosworth and Charles Sullivan, both of whom had studied at the Pennsylvania Academy of the Fine Arts. In 1841, Sullivan arranged Spencer's first exhibition at the church rectory. The success of the exhibition prompted Nicholas Longworth, a benefactor of several successful artists in Cincinnati, including Thomas Read, William Henry Powell, and Hiram Powers, to offer similar patronage to the young girl. Her father recognized her talent but refused Longworth's support, insisting that he remain her guardian. In the fall of 1841, the family moved to Cincinnati, where Lilly remained for the next seven years. Upon her arrival, Longworth offered her a chance to study the Old Masters on a seven-year tour of Europe; again she refused his patronage, preferring to remain in America. While her father sought pupils for French lessons, Spencer painted numerous portrait commissions and worked on "fancy pieces" with local landscape and portrait painter James Beard. Her determination was foreign to Cincinnati's gender-biased community, which generally frowned on women seeking professions. Her marriage to Englishman Benjamin Rush Spencer freed her to pursue her artistic interests. In 1848, the Spencers moved to New York, where she exhibited at the American Art-Union and the National Academy of Design while continuing to show her work in Cincinnati. She formed associations with the Western Art Union and the French firm Goupil, Vibert & Company, which commissioned her to execute popular prints of literary subjects and sentimental genre scenes. Ever aware of her family's financial needs, she bowed to the trends of the country and turned almost exclusively to nostalgic depictions of familial harmony. In 1858, the Spencers moved to Newark, New Jersey, and rented a house from her most important patron, Marcus L. Ward, a successful businessman from an old and prominent Newark family. Her time away from New York was detrimental to her career, and in 1867, Spencer returned in the hope of reviving her career. Her old dealer, Samuel Avery, noted that her paintings had improved since her last exhibition in New York but stated that his clients were not interested in American art but in "the great foreign names."[1] A newspaper columnist in St. Louis paid homage to her many accomplishments and success:

> ***Let Men . . . know that with the skill of her hands and the power of her head, she sustains a family . . . . Aye, sustains them a thousandfold better than she could have done with the needle or the washtub, and gives out to the world besides the rich treasures which become the rays of sunshine in many a heart and home.***[2]

*Our Future Americans* is a posthumous allegorical portrait of Catherine (1849-1860) and Francis (1856-1864) Ward.[3] Spencer's work reflects Ward's nationalistic dedication by depicting his two children as embodiments of their country's ideals. Francis is painted as a young patriot with a drum and an American flag. Catherine fulfills her role as a proper young lady: one hand rests on her strand of pearls while the other tames the parrot perched on the stand. Their serious expressions and detached gazes, however, belie the playful spirit of childhood.

---

1 Biographical information taken from Robin Bolton Smith, *Lilly Martin Spencer 1822-1902: The Joys of Sentiment,* Exhib. cat. (Washington, D.C.: Smithsonian Institution Press, 1973).

2 Gage, "Mrs. L.M. Spencer, the Artist," in unidentified St. Louis newspaper, ca. 1854-1857, quoted in ibid., 76.

3 Spencer executed numerous portraits of the Ward family in exchange for a rental option on a house in Newark owned by Ward.

# *Lucy May Stanton*

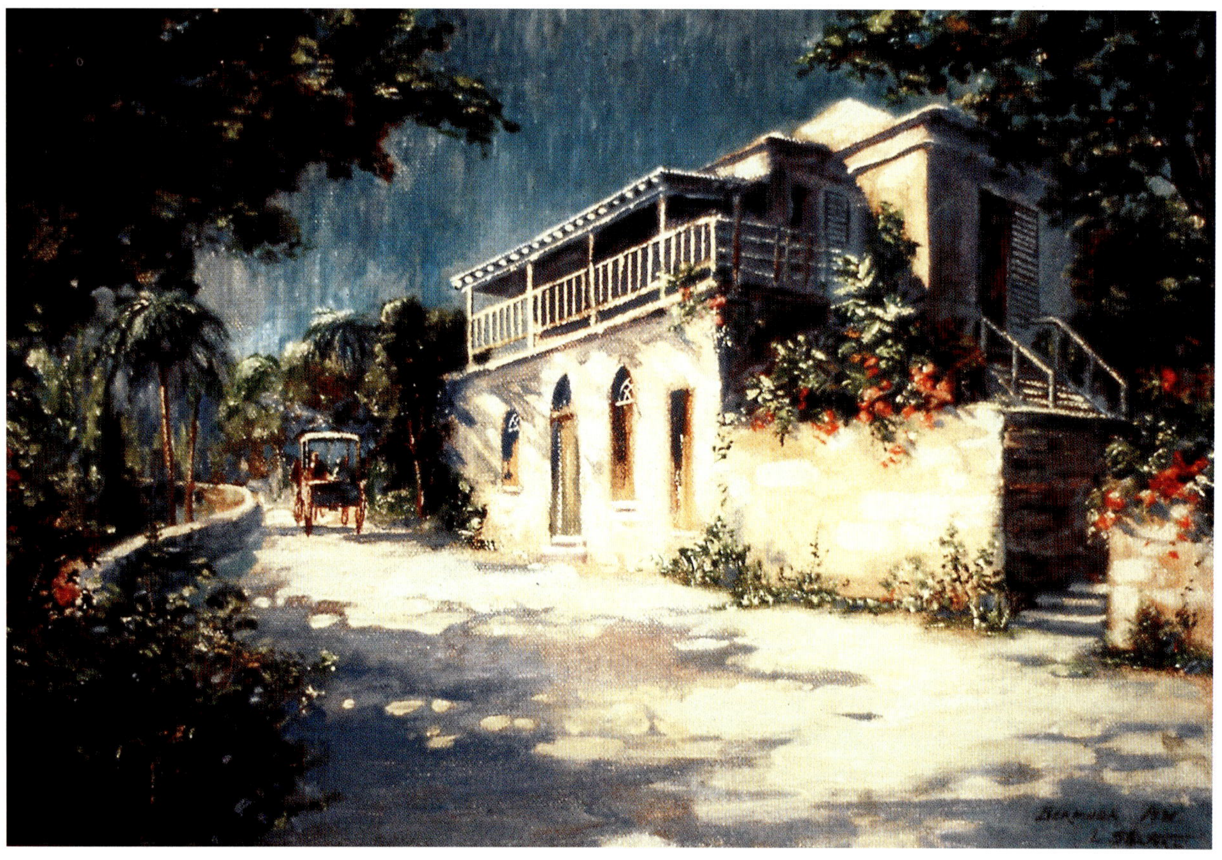

**No. 46**

LUCY MAY STANTON (AMERICAN, 1876-1931)
*Bermuda*, 1925
Oil on canvas
11 ½ x 17 ½ inches
The Sellars Collection

BORN AND RAISED IN ATLANTA, Lucy May Stanton began her studies at a young age under the French painter Madame Sally Seago in New Orleans. Stanton's father, a successful businessman and founder of the Southern Baptist College for Women in Atlanta, amply provided for his daughter and actively promoted her artistic interests. In 1889, the Stanton family traveled abroad, where Lucy was exposed to the masters of European art in London, Paris, Rome, Naples, Venice, Vienna, Antwerp, and Amsterdam. Upon her return, Stanton enrolled at her father's school and studied with James Field, a painter who had trained at the Académie Julian. Inspired by her initial experience abroad, she returned to Paris after graduation. By 1898, Stanton was back in Georgia, where she taught at the Y.M.C.A., maintained a successful studio at the Grande Opera House in downtown Atlanta, and exhibited her work in Philadelphia and New York. After teaching briefly in Los Angeles in 1904, Stanton traveled to Europe to work in Paris and Amsterdam. She returned once again to Georgia, where she opened a studio in Athens. By 1913, Stanton had increasingly withdrawn from her patrons, family, and critics and had moved to the remote village of Valley Town in the Smoky Mountains. She wrote in her diary, "Life becomes so crowded with facts–with events in the towns–that it is well to spend a year away in the mountains in order to turn over the facts and have time to digest them and learn one's lessons and to apply them. Here in these mountains with other obstructions or attractions removed one works with glowing delight."[1] Rejuvenated from her self-imposed solitude, she resumed her travels and moved to Boston in 1916, near her beloved summer retreat in Ogunquit, Maine. Stanton moved to Athens in 1926, where she spent the last six years of her life.

Primarily known for her miniature portraits, Stanton also painted small landscapes and genre scenes. Completed after a short trip to Bermuda in 1924, the present painting demonstrates Stanton's ability to lend a sense of poetic grandeur to even the most intimate compositions. The resort town is presented as a picturesque landscape dappled in sunlight and enlivened by a brilliant palette. The horse and carriage that emerge from the wooded background suggest a simple life, uninhabited by industry or urban restlessness. Indeed, resort areas like Bermuda were known for their ability to heal weary city dwellers, and their popularity steadily increased in the twentieth century as leisure time and vacations became more accessible to middle-class workers.

1 Biographical information taken from W. Stanton Forbes, *Lucy M. Stanton, Artist* (Atlanta: Emory University Press, 1975).

# Gilbert Stuart

GILBERT STUART, SON OF A Scottish-born tobacco laborer, first lived near Narragansett Bay in what became Rhode Island. When Stuart was six, his family moved to Newport. He initially studied under the Scottish painter Cosimo Alexander and traveled as his assistant through the southern colonies seeking portrait commissions. He briefly continued his studies with Alexander in Edinburgh but returned home penniless after his mentor's death in 1772. By studying portraits by successful Colonial painters Robert Feke, John Singleton Copley, and Joseph Blackburn, Stuart slowly developed his own style of searching realism and simplified compositions that characterized his mature work. Stuart, encouraged by the success of Benjamin West and Copley in London, traveled there in 1775, after the outbreak of the Revolutionary War in Boston. Desperate for work and nearly starving, Stuart called upon the kindness of West, who had recently been hired as the official history painter to George III. Initially hired as a copyist in West's studio, Stuart soon became his principal assistant. He learned quickly both from his teacher and from West's British associates Sir Joshua Reynolds, Thomas Gainsborough, and George Romney. After the successful debut of *The Skater* (National Gallery of Art, Washington, D.C.) at the Royal Academy exhibition of 1782, Stuart set up his own studio and began fulfilling numerous portrait commissions. Although he was never short of work, Stuart's extravagant style of living, coupled with a new wife and baby, drained him of his savings. He fled to Dublin, where his situation did not improve; finally, Stuart set sail for America in 1793. A new urgency and purpose had overtaken America since Stuart had left twenty years earlier. He first settled in New York but moved to Philadelphia late in 1795,

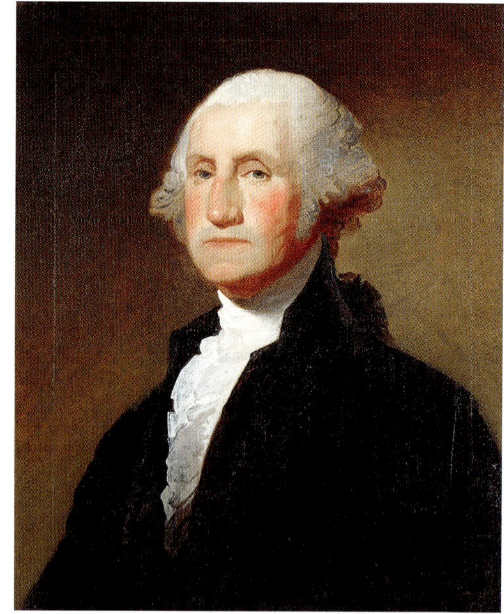

**No. 47**

GILBERT STUART (AMERICAN, 1755-1828)
*George Washington*
Oil on canvas
29 x 22 ¼ inches
Collection of Mark and Lynn McConnell

all the while planning to paint the definitive portrait of the country's hero and first president, George Washington. The first artist to paint Washington from life was Charles Willson Peale, in 1772. In the numerous portraits that he did of Washington, before and during his presidency, Peale depicted him as a symbol, mainly as a general during the Revolutionary War. Numerous artists followed Peale, including Colonel John Trumbull and Edward Savage, but the most famous images were completed during Washington's second term as president. Most notable among these and the images reproduced the most are those by Gilbert Stuart and Rembrandt Peale. Actually, Stuart was granted two sittings. The first, in 1794 or 1795, produced the "Vaughan type," an example of which is in the National Gallery of Art, Washington, D.C. The second resulted in the "Atheneum type," done first in the spring of 1796, which shows the left side of the president's face.[1] Stuart spent the next several years producing copies of the three popular portraits, over one hundred of which are known to exist.[2] Though Stuart showed himself capable of such iconic masterpieces as these, by 1800 he was increasingly overcome with debilitating lethargy and depression, partially due to his excessive drinking. After a brief stay in Washington, Stuart moved to Boston, where he continued to paint until his death in 1828.[3]

Stuart assumed a difficult task when he decided to paint the definitive portrait of Washington. He had no American artistic precedent to rely upon, and very few European examples existed of leaders outside of the role of military victor or king. Stuart's challenge to create an iconic presence was further complicated by Washington's unheroic physique and awkward features as well as his unwillingness to allow a glimpse at his inner character. While he needed to present an idealized image, the artist could not sacrifice the individual likeness expected of eighteenth-century portraiture. The resulting "Atheneum type" depicted an older Washington who, with a broadened jaw due to incorrectly fitted false wooden teeth, shows the tremendous strain of his many years as general and then as president. Stuart was struck by the president's plain attire and painted him in a black coat with a modest white ruffle at the neck. Stuart's success comes from the flourishing brushwork that gives energy and nobility to Washington's face without making him seem aloof. He claimed that the background should only be used to enhance the gaze and expression of the sitter. Although Stuart believed that he failed "to elicit the expression he knew must accord with such features and such a man," Americans considered the portrait an excellent likeness and awarded Stuart dozens of commissions for copies.[4]

---

1 There is a third type, the "Lansdowne type," which is a standing figure based on the "Atheneum type," an example of which is in the Pennsylvania Academy of the Fine Arts. The other source for the "Lansdowne type" is the Roman sculpture *Augustus of Prima Porta.*

2 Mantle Fielding and John H. Morgan, *Life Portraits of Washington and Their Replicas* (Philadelphia, 1939); according to Morgan and Fielding, there are over 450 "life" portraits of Washington.

3 Biographical material taken from Richard McLanathan, *Gilbert Stuart* (New York: Harry N. Abrams, Inc., 1986); Michael Quick, *American Portraiture in the Grand Manner: 1720- 1920* (Los Angeles: Los Angeles County Museum, 1981); and Theodore E. Stebbins, Jr., *A New World: Masterpieces of American Painting 1760-1910* (Boston: Museum of Fine Arts, 1983), 203.

4 McLanathan, 83.

# Allen Tucker

ALLEN TUCKER GRADUATED from the Columbia University of Mines in 1888 and practiced architecture for over fifteen years with the firm of McIlvaine and Tucker. He also studied at the Art Students League under John Henry Twachtman throughout the 1890s and often traveled to Europe, where he joined other expatriate artists Robert Henri, Louis-Paul Dessar, Charles Fromuth, Charles Grafly, and Edward Redfield. His friendship with Henri resulted in his inclusion in the exhibition of the Independents in 1910. Tucker became a founding member of the Association of American Painters and Sculptors, which organized the Armory Show of 1913. The radical nature of the European Cubist and Fauvist works showcased at the exhibition prompted many American artists to depart from the commercial and critical safety net of Impressionism and delve into European Post-Impressionism and other emerging styles. Tucker similarly abandoned his earlier Impressionist style and began to experiment with pure color, loose brushwork, and a heavily impastoed surface. His mature Post-Impressionist manner reflects the strong influence of Vincent van Gogh, whose style Tucker emulated throughout his career. His work was critically praised and exhibited regularly at the National Academy of Design (1905-10), the Pennsylvania Academy of the Fine Arts (1904-39), the Whitney Museum of American Art (1918-39), and the Corcoran Gallery of Art (1910-36).[1]

Nicknamed the "Van Gogh of America," Tucker focused most of his compositions on the secluded countrysides of Maine and Massachusetts as well as those of Italy and France. Like Van Gogh, Tucker preferred themes of solitude and isolation and favored broad, robust expanses of meadowland and mountain scenery in which the elements of nature expressed a palpable energy. *October Shadows*, presenting nature as a formidable power, relegates human presence to a rustic barn partially shielded by trees. While figures have been eliminated, Tucker creates human-like forms within the swaying shrubbery and large, animated trees. He energizes his composition through bold juxtapositions of contrasting forms–foreground to background, dark to light–that have a dynamism drawn from his virile brushwork. Tucker is unusual in prewar American painting because his works are so openly expressionistic, with an awkwardness of forms suggestive of the contemporary work of Arthur Dove.

---

1 Biographical information taken from "Allen Tucker and Van Gogh," *The Art Digest* 7 (15 February 1933): 14; "American Van Gogh," *The Art Digest* 22 (15 October 1947): 19; and Forbes Watson, *Allen Tucker*, Exhib. cat. (New York: Whitney Museum of American Art, 1932).

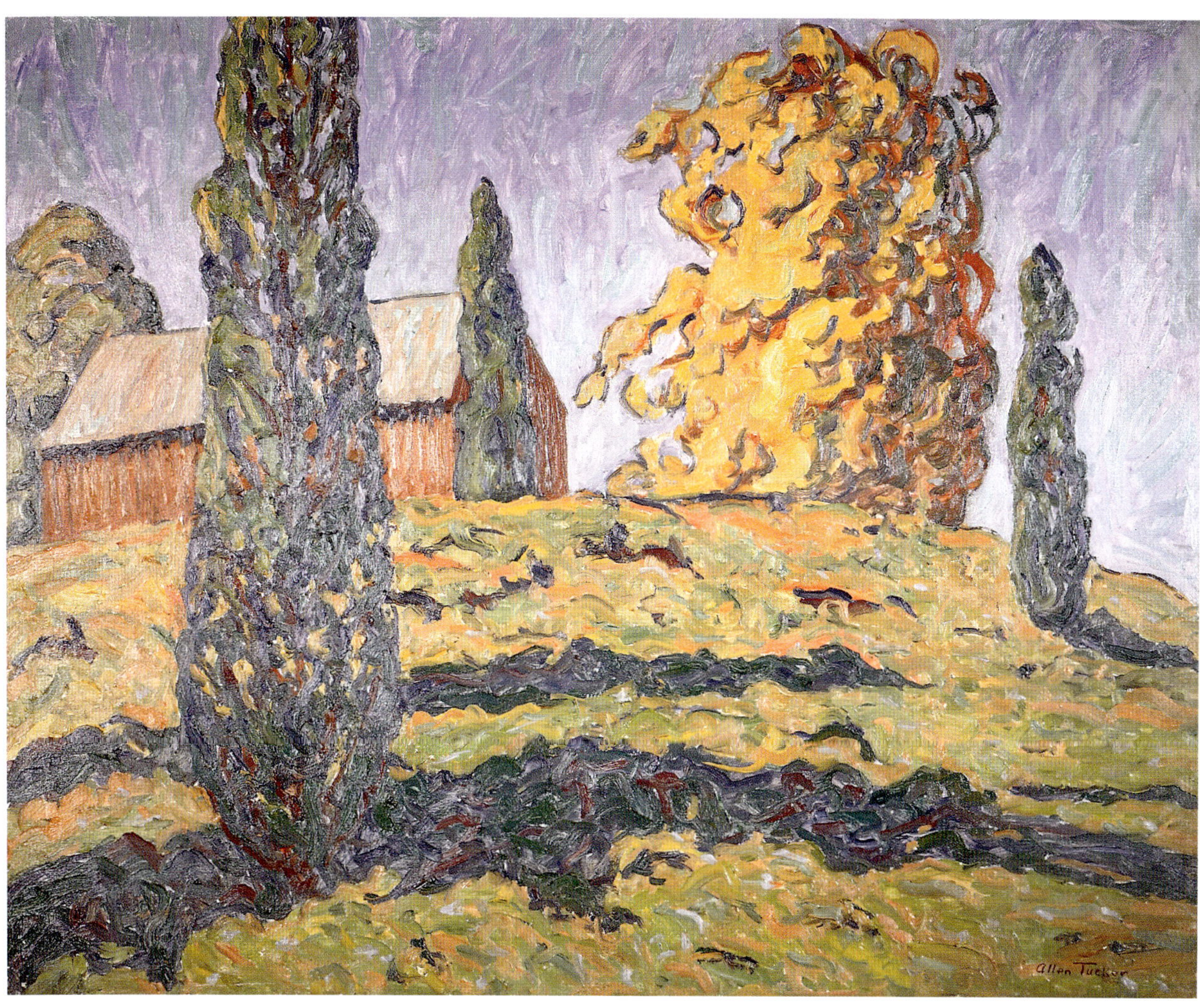


~ **No. 48** ~

ALLEN TUCKER (AMERICAN, 1866-1939)
*October Shadows*, ca. 1918
Oil on canvas
40 x 50 inches
Collection of Stephen and Linda Sessler

# *Elihu Vedder*

Elihu Vedder's peripatetic life began in his youth, which he spent traveling between his birthplace of New York, his father's adopted home of Cuba, and his grandfather's farm in upstate New York. He formed attachments to each of these three very different locales. Vedder's artistic training began in New York under the genre and history painter Tompkins H. Matteson. Anxious to explore the more exotic terrain of Europe, Vedder departed from America in 1856 for Paris, where he studied briefly under the academic painter François-Edouard Picot. A year later, he joined a group of young, non-conformist artists in Florence known as the Macchiaioli, who were revolting against the staid academic traditions of Italian art. Vedder's early work embraced the reductive palette and spontaneous brushstroke promoted by the group. While his American counterparts

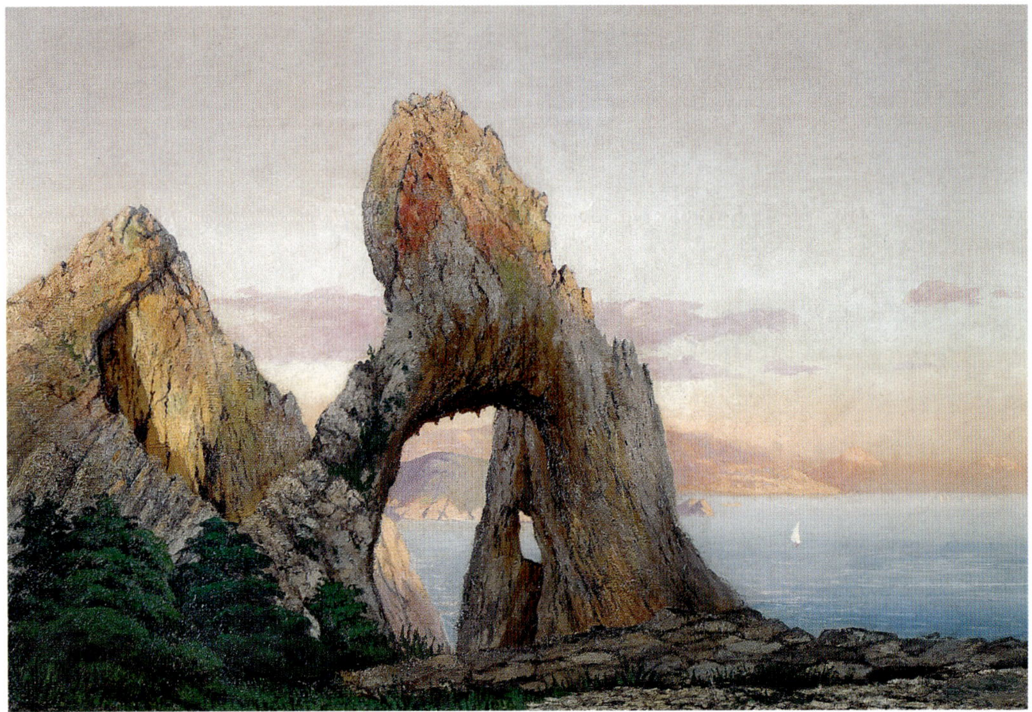

**No. 49**

Elihu Vedder (American 1836-1923), *Capri*, 1908.
Oil on canvas, 35 x 50 inches. Collection of Beverly Hart Bremer.

painted the vistas of Florence, Vedder and his colleagues preferred the unexplored reaches of the Tuscan countryside. Due to his lack of money, Vedder reluctantly returned to New York in 1861 and remained in the city, except for brief visits to Boston, until the conclusion of the Civil War. It was a productive time for Vedder, who quickly became a part of the lively, self-styled Bohemian group of writers and artists active in the city. Two of his most significant works from these years, *The Questioner of the Sphynx* (Boston Museum of Fine Arts) and *Lair of the Sea Serpent* (Boston Museum of Fine Arts), were exhibited at the National Academy of Design in 1864. A year later, Vedder's provocative style of Romantic classicism was recognized with a full membership in the Academy. The artist's penchant for mystery was expressed in his book *Digressions of V*: "It is their unwritten meaning, their poetic meaning, far more eloquent than words can express; and it sometimes seemed to me that this impression would be chilled or lessened by a greater unveiling of their mysteries, and that to me Isis unveiled would be Isis dead." [1] Vedder returned to Italy via Paris in 1866; the varied topography of his adopted home inspired a new series of small landscapes. Whether executed *en plein air* or in his studio, his detailed landscapes sacrificed topographic accuracy for an evocative mysticism which had become the hallmark of his style. As Joshua Taylor stated, "specificity belongs to the fabricated part, the remembered impression is that relating to nature."[2] After ten years abroad, Vedder returned to New York in 1879 and participated in the growing decorative arts movement. He produced designs for decorative items such as stained glass, tiles, and firebacks, and illustrations for greeting cards and magazine covers. While he returned often to America over the next few decades, Vedder made his home in Italy. He spent his late years in Rome and Capri and continued to paint until his death at the age of eighty-seven.[3]

After many visits to Capri, a long-time haunt of international artists, Vedder designed and built a home overlooking the Bay of Naples. Inspired by the romantic beauty of the island, he returned to the evocative art of landscape painting. Impressive in scale, *Capri* depicts nature with the overtly dramatic palette and enigmatic emotion characteristic of Vedder. The composition, while different from earlier works, relies upon his repertoire of Italian landscape elements. The anthropomorphic rock formation dominating the composition recalls the Italian ruins of the Roman campagna, and the sense of deep perspective with distant, sunlit mountains and a lone sailboat recalls the numerous sketches of Bordighera he executed in the early 1870s. Finding its roots in Vedder's imagination, *Capri* evokes a time inhabited by myth and untouched by industry.

---

1 Elihu Vedder, *The Digressions of V* (Boston: Houghton Mifflin Company, 1910), 451, cited in Joshua C. Taylor, "Perceptions and Digressions," in *Perceptions and Evocations: The Art of Elihu Vedder* (Washington, D.C.: Smithsonian Institution Press, 1979), 61.

2 Taylor, 91.

3 Biographical information taken from Regina Soria, *Elihu Vedder: American Visionary Artist in Rome (1836-1923)* (Rutherford: Fairleigh Dickinson University Press, 1970); and ibid.

# *Worthington Whittredge*

THOMAS WORTHINGTON WHITTREDGE'S interest in nature began at an early age on his family farm outside Springfield, Ohio. At seventeen, he moved to Cincinnati to apprentice with his brother-in-law's house- and sign-painting company and pursue his interest in formal art on his own. He experimented unsuccessfully with commercial daguerreotypes and portraiture; after these businesses failed, Whittredge returned to Cincinnati to devote himself exclusively to landscape painting. The scenic beauty of the Ohio River valley inspired Whittredge, who painted under the well-known Romantic influence of Thomas Cole and Thomas Doughty, i.e., the Hudson River school. Although Cincinnati had evolved into a leading cultural center by mid-century, Whittredge was convinced that a tour of Europe was necessary to complete his education. In 1849, he joined fellow Americans in Düsseldorf and worked with landscape painters Andreas Achenbach and Johann Schirmer and history painter Wilhelm Schadow. The Düsseldorf school promoted large, highly finished studio landscapes that liberally reinterpreted nature for compositional effect while describing it in minute detail. Motivated by artistic restlessness and a desire to see Rome, Whittredge traveled via Switzerland to Italy, where he joined painter Frederic Edwin Church and writer Nathaniel Hawthorne in an American artists' colony. Upon his return to the United States in 1859, Whittredge set up a studio in New York. Characterizing this time as "the most crucial period of my life," he noted the importance of creating a distinctly American landscape within his art: "We are looking and hoping for something distinctive in the art of our country, something which shall receive a new tinge from our peculiar form of government, from our position on the globe, or something peculiar to our people, to distinguish it from the art of the other nations and to enable us to pronounce without shame the oft-repeated phrase, 'American Art.'"[1] He was elected an academician of the National Academy of Design in 1862 and served as its president from 1874 through 1877. During this period, he traveled to the West, where his landscapes began to reflect the influence of the Barbizon school of painters to whom he had been first exposed in Europe.[2] As he immersed himself in nature, Whittredge's style began to evolve from the earlier panoramic vision of the Hudson River school to a more personal vision of the forest interior.

*Flood on the Delaware* depicts a farmer harvesting pumpkins after a rainstorm has flooded his field. Characteristic of Whittredge's forest interiors, this painting represents the nostalgic charm of an arcadian rural scene. Although his late style vacillated between the Hudson River school and the newly popular Barbizon school style, an adept handling of light, impressive use of detail, and thematic harmony of man and nature continued to typify his oeuvre late into his career. Along with Homer Dodge Martin and Asher B. Durand, Whittredge turned landscape painting into an intimate, personal expression of light and atmosphere. In 1880, S.G.W. Benjamin acknowledged Whittredge's success in his publication *Art in America*: "[Whittredge's] landscapes are thoroughly individual and American .... As a faithful delineator of the various phases of American wood interiors, Mr. Whittredge has deservedly won a permanent place in the popular favor."[3] Often, these forest interiors carry a religious significance, indicating the contemplative mood associated with church interiors, and by extension the gentler, feminine side of human nature. The subdued color, balanced composition, and flow of light-dark patterns from foreground to background are further indications of how far American landscape painters such as Whittredge had moved from the sublime visions of earlier American artists.

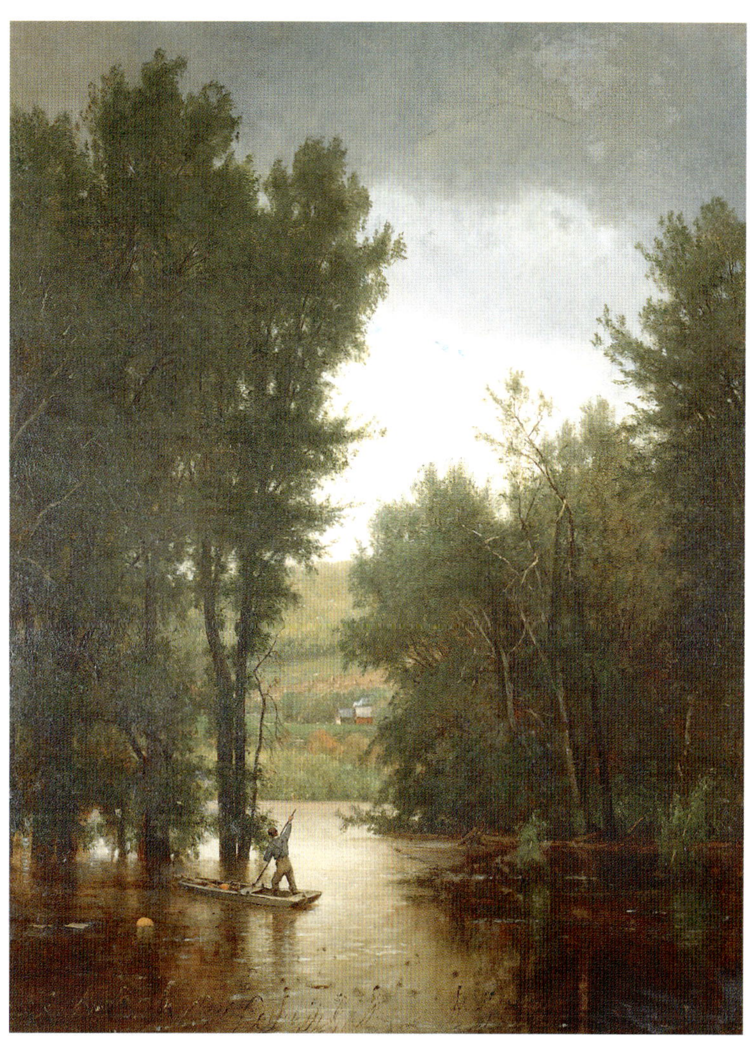

**No. 50**

WORTHINGTON WHITTREDGE (AMERICAN, 1820-1910)
*Flood on the Delaware*, 1880
Oil on canvas
34 x 26 ½ inches
Collection of Mr. and Mrs. Fred D. Bentley, Sr.

---

1 Quoted in John I.H. Bauer, ed., "The Autobiography of Worthington Whittredge, 1820-1910," *Brooklyn Museum Journal* (1942; reprinted, New York: Arno Press Inc., 1969), 39-40.

2 Biographical material taken from Bauer; Cheryl Cibulka, *Quiet Places: The American Landscape of Worthington Whittredge* (Washington, D.C.: Garamond Pridemark Press, 1982); and Anthony F. Janson, *Worthington Whittredge* (Cambridge: Cambridge University Press, 1989).

3 S.G.W. Benjamin, *Art in America; A Critical and Historical Sketch* (New York: Harper & Bros., 1880), 73.

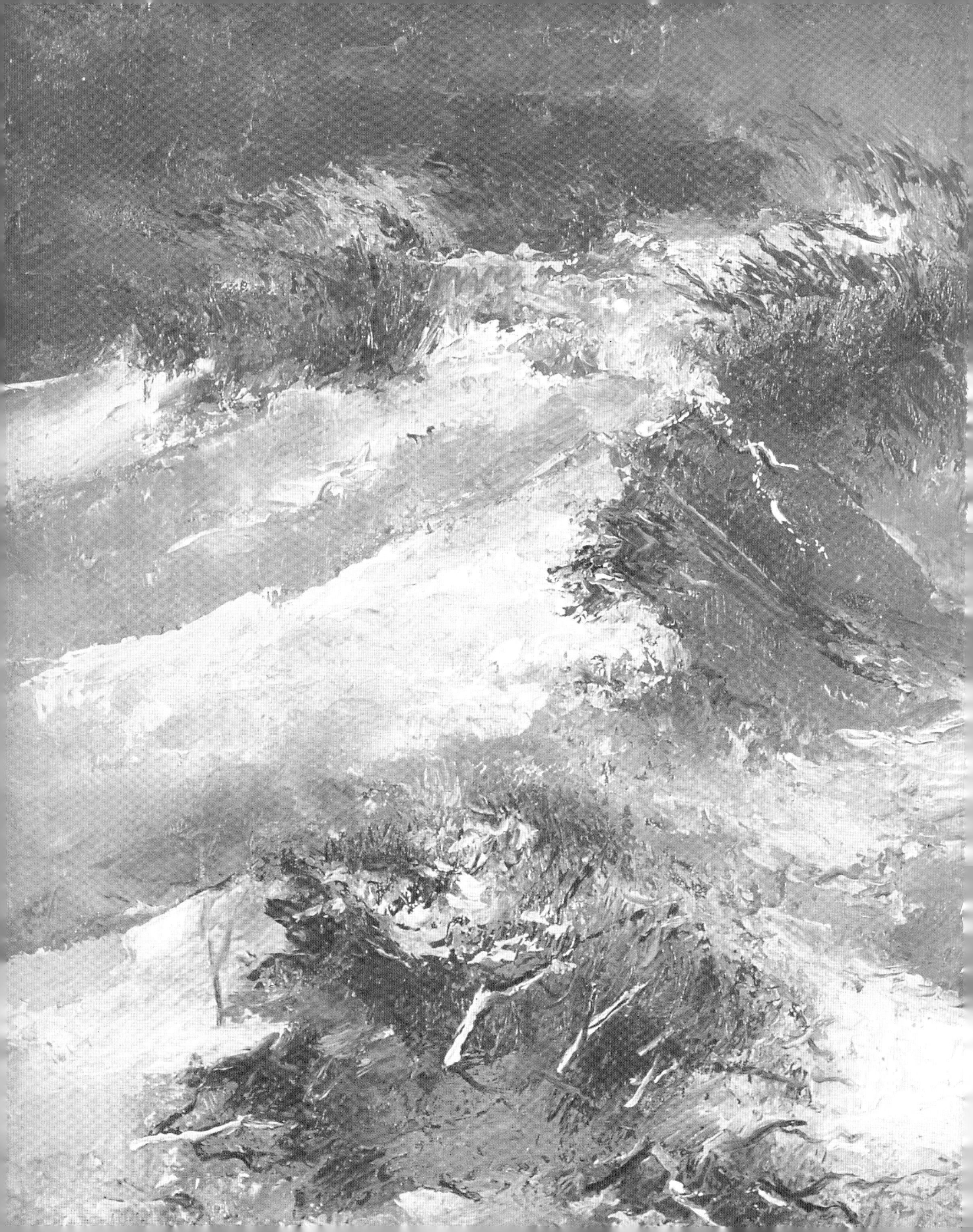